The **Ultimate** Answering **M a c h i n e** *Message* Book

The **Ultimate Answering Machine Message** Book

Marnie Winston-Macauley
with contributions from Alan Garner
and Warren Farrell

Andrews McMeel Publishing

Kansas City

ISBN: 0-8362-3225-9

Library of Congress Catalog Card Number: 96–79730

Book design and composition by Top Dog Design
Click Art © TMaker.

ATTENTION: SCHOOLS AND BUSINESSES

Andrews and McMeel books are available at quantity discounts with bulk purchase for educational, business, or sales promotional use. For information, please write to: Special Sales Department, Andrews and McMeel, 4520 Main Street, Kansas City, Missouri 64111.

DEDICATION

For Dr. Robert U. Akeret who,
with infinite love, skill, and creativity,
continues to teach so many the
"meaning" beyond the "message."

ACKNOWLEDGMENTS

As always, to "the man"—Alan Garner. Thanks too to Warren Farrell for his contributions. Then the "tag team" at Andrews and McMeel, Tom Thornton, Dorothy O'Brien, Stephanie Bennett, Eden Blackwood, Allan Stark, Polly Blair, and, of course, Hugh Andrews. And love too to my personal "tag team." They are Dr. Joshua and Jill Winston . . . "and Justus," Terry Lester, Stephanie Winston, John H. Johnson, Dr. Albert Stanek, Barr Seitz, Charles and Mary Keating, Rita Lloyd, Allyson Rice-Taylor, Julie Poll, Marta Sanders, Laurence and Pat Caso, Jonathan Macauley, Scott Holmes, Tom Wiggin, and Walter Engels.

Huge hugs to Craig Kelso, Jeremy Leaf, and Hannah Westby—always in my thoughts.

Plus a very special word of love to Mary Rader—a very special woman in our lives.

And then there are "the two" who (alas) *never* answer the phone at our house. My husband, Ian T. Macauley and our son Simon Louis Winston-Macauley. *Hey you guys, Mom is leaving a message. . . . Will you pick up*? PLEASE?! *Hello*? **HELLOO?**

CONTENTS

INTRODUCTION

When my colleague and dear friend Alan Garner approached me with this project I thought, "Interesting, but does the world really need another book on answering device messages?" Plus, I was busy promoting my other projects, putting the finishing touches on new books, and dispensing advice to my "Cyber-Hearts" for ABC *Love On Line* and AOL's Entertainment Channel.

But the material kept calling me. One day, I locked my office door and gave it a major "think." What the heck makes these messages and machines so potentially fascinating and funny? After two aspirins and a Tums chaser (not to mention missing three episodes of *Seinfeld* reruns), I mumbled "Eureka" and crawled into bed with what we used to call, when I was writing *As the World Turns*, a POV (Point of View).

Why are these devilish little messages so intriguing, clever, hysterical, or just plain *nuts*? Because, like the "Kiss Me If You're Bosnian" and "I Brake For Bison" bumper stickers before them, they allow us to "connect" without (too many) consequences. We can relate, share, and yes, even bond— we can tickle, trash, treat, and trick—by tape, and walk away with our teeth intact. ("Hey. It was a joke, pal!") And if we don't like the responses, no nasty, gut-twisting encounters, no awkward angst, no messy migraine moments. Nope! Long-distance "messagering" beats "up close and personal" for saying our peace and our poison . . . all through the safety of a little plastic box. So each message becomes a mini-personality-profile. A teeny, tiny corner of creative communication that is uniquely ours—unexcerpted, unedited, and unexpurgated. A golden opportunity to speak out and be counted. And of course, there's always the erase button!

It's with this POV that I wrote this book. While each message is specific to the character I was creating, please feel free to improvise (okay, steal) for your own personal use. Should you have any questions, don't hesitate to call me, as I no doubt will be basking on a beach in Tahiti with the profits I made because you bought this book—leave a message after the beep. Oh . . . and please don't hang up! I can't stand hang ups! True, it could be you. But it could have been the Pulitzer Prize Committee . . . or Oliver Stone asking me to write his next screenplay . . . and I'll never know. Wait a minute. It could be a burglar . . . or the IRS . . or my mother-in-law . . . or . . . on second thought . . . my partner . . . or my publisher .   . or better yet—**BEEP**!!

Mankind and Machine:

Wrinkles from the World to the Wires

TAPE-A-PHOBIA

This is Polly. You've reached my machine because I won't pick up. Sorry, but I refuse to expose myself to unnecessary risks from talking into plastic telephone hardware which no doubt emits hidden, dangerous ions that can cause cancer or Alzheimer's. Therefore, leave a message and I will e-mail you from my office computer—at Three Mile Island.
BEEP.

HUMAN MALFUNCTION

Message One

Hi, guys! Yep! Got a machine! About time, right? And I thought this gizmo would be hard to work. Piece a cake! I just put this in and hit "record." Then, *after* I record my message, I press this doohinky to **STOP** it, and—
BEEP.

Message Two

Hi, guys! YEP, ME again. Guess I screwed up a little. OKAY. Piece of cake. Just put this in and hit "record." Then, *after* I record my message, I press *this* other doohinky to STOP it, then JUST talk *normally* to—
BEEP.

Message Three

Yeah, me *again*! Okey-dokey. Now . . . just put this thing in . . . hit "record." Then, *after* I record my message, I press this other doohinky . . . to *stop* it, then just talk **normally** for thirty seconds 'til I hear the BEEP . . . right? So . . . where's that BEEP? No BEEP yet? Damn! Helloooooooooo???? Listen . . . if you can . . . *hear* me . . . write me a G-DDAMN . . . LETTER!!!

I DON'T GET NO RESPECT

This is Russell. Leave a message at the BEEP. What? *Boring*, you say? Well, you have no one to blame but *yourself*! I've left *fifteen clever messages* and not **ONE** of you had the decency to say "Wow! Cool message!" Who am I? Jerry Seinfeld? **DO I NEED THIS?** I think not. So . . . just leave your ungrateful message after the **BEEP.**

On second thought, *don't bother*! I'm changing my number and leaving a **NEW**, hysterically funny message—and YOU won't hear it! **BEEP.**

DOUBLY WIRED
(Mechanical Voice)

This is Ray's computer's answering device. I'm either booting up or on-line so we *can't* hook up. Just leave your e-mail address, and I'll download you as soon as my modem's free—or meet me in the Hot 'n' Horny chat room at ten. **BEEP.**

HAVE I GOT A BARGAIN FOR YOU!

Hiya! Yup! Finally broke open the ol' piggy bank and sprung for this machine. None of your fancy jobs. Oh, no! Not for Sherm. Stole this little beauty for a song—$9.99—down on Wharf and Canal. Outdoor stand . . . SO . . . leave you . . . number—*&%$#** I get back fr . . . beach with . . . Metal detec . . . &%$#@—GET BACK . . . YOU . **Hey,** so LONG as GETS . . . JOB DONE, RIGHT? **Right?**
BEEP . . . Beep BEEP?

I DARE YOU

You've reached the Galloping Poll Institute. Our statistics show that out of one thousand tape-recorded messages, only 372 Americans leave an appropriate response. In our quest to provide objective, statistical information, the Institute will be recording what *you* do. Will you be among that brave minority of mature human beings who respond responsibly? Or will you be one of the *others*? *One of the 628 wimps, cowards, and sniveling slime who hang up or leave tasteless and tacky messages? Well? What's it gonna be, hotshot?*
BEEP.

Sex by Wire:

Mating and Dating Calls

STUD DUD

This message is just for YOU, *babe*. You were special from day one, *sweetcakes*. But last night—totally, unforgettably, awesome! Get back to you ASAP, *doll*. Just tell me where you are . . . and don't forget to leave your NAME, since I LOST the **matchbook cover** I wrote it on.
BEEP.

LUSTY GRANNY

(Elderly Female Voice)

Hello. You've reached Millicent Kravitz at the Happydale Home for the Aged. If you are that **NASTY** young man who *insists* on making those **LEWD** and lascivious **OBSCENE** calls, please stop *immediately* . . . until I return from the Bingo room. Then perhaps we can continue our little discussion . . . before I take my teeth out for nap time.
BEEP.

IN NEED OF COMMITMENT

Hi. You've reached Henry. If it's Myrna, *you're right*. After eight years, it's TIME I got over my fear of commitment and moved in with you. But there are a few **DETAILS** we should straighten out—nothing major. First, *clothes*. No sense dragging them **ALL** over, so except for a few shirts and a pair of jeans, I'm leaving most of them with my mother, along with my electric shaver. Don't worry about razors, I'll bring the *disposable*

kind. Now . . . *the tuna fish.* I bought a case on sale. **No problem**, I've marked each can with India ink so we know whose fish is whose. I'm down getting a red marker from the super, so you can label YOURS, before I FAX the rest of the list. Well, that's about it. Can't tell you what a great feeling it is *now that I've finally licked that commitment problem*!
BEEP.

HEY, I'VE GOT MY PRIDE!

(Mechanical Voice: Saturday, 9:50 P.M.)

You've reached Gloria and I'm *unavailable*. **WHAT?** You thought I'd be *sitting here*, all dressed up, just WAITING for you to call and ask *me* out—on Saturday? Well you can **FORGET IT!** Now YOU can wait while I take *my* sweet time to get back to *you*!
BEEP.

DIRTY OLD TAPE

(IN MISTER ROGERS'S VOICE)

Hi. I can't come to the telephone right now because I'm **cruising** my neighborhood—looking for ACTION. That's right. "**ACTION.**" That's an "A" word—like "Animal." And when I FIND some . . . I'm going to go to a **HOTEL**. THAT'S an "H" word . . . like "**HOT**". Can YOU think of OTHER "H" words? If you CAN, leave them, plus any other **NAUGHTY** words after the BEEP.
BEEP.

SO TELL ME ALL ABOUT HOW YOU FEEL . . . ABOUT ME!

Hi. This is Gary. If this is Reneé . . . some blind date we had last night, *right*? I talked for what . . . six hours straight? And never *once* got bored. But it occurred to me, we didn't get a whole lot of time to talk about *you*. So I've devised a little pop quiz to learn more about how you feel! Just press one through four on your key-pad with your answer. Here goes, babe!

Question One:

I feel GARY is *most* interesting when he's talking about: 1) his ex; 2) his Mom; 3) his therapist; 4) his tuba.

Question Two:

I felt the *most* fascinating part of GARY'S life was:
1) age one through three—"the age of block mastery";
2) age fourteen through thirty—"the autoerotic era";
3) age thirty-one through thirty-six—"the awakening";
4) age thirty-seven to present—"the civil service years."

Question Three:

I feel GARY's *best* feature is: 1) his brilliant conversation; 2) his ability to cry for hours openly in front of a woman; 3) his sensitivity; 4) his awareness.

No rush! Just fill out this quiz *before* we make plans for our *next* terrific date—hopefully, as soon as you get back from that sudden trip to Cartanga . . . which, for some reason, I can't seem to locate on my—**BEEP!**

SAFE SEX

(Female Voice)

Hello. You've reached Box No. 3765. If you're responding to my personal ad, please leave your name, the
date of your LAST BLOOD TEST, and the number of
the laboratory. You will receive a *release form*, which you
MUST sign and return to me. Pending the results, I
will contact you by mail to discuss the **NEXT TEN
STEPS**. But remember, I *must* receive a certified
photocopy of your hospital records *before* we engage
in any further contact.

BEEP!

EVEN SAFER SEX

Hi there. You've reached Jan. If you're the single guy
I talked to for *hours* during the charity drive yesterday,
I think you're incredible, too! The most intelligent,
attractive man I've talked to in ages! And I agree, I
would like to take it further—*much* further, **NOW!** So
. . . if you put your lips close to the receiver, I'll do the
same—and *together* we'll IGNITE in ***passion.*** And
perhaps one day, in the future, we can actually meet
in person, *Reverend.*

BEEP.

Tell Me
Another!

Liars and Other Losers

ALL THIS AND A CUBIC ZIRCONIA TOO!

You've reached our Prize Control Headquarters! CONGRATULATIONS! That's right! As our certified letter stated, *your* number was selected—*along with six million others*—totally at RANDOM, making *you* a bona fide winner! To claim *your* prize, valued at—*from one dollar to*—fifty thousand dollars, all *you* have to do is enter—*your credit card number*—and press the pound sign now! That will entitle you to collect your prize at our international headquarters—*in Bosnia . . . after you tour our lovely time-shares.* As an *extra* bonus, we will arrange air travel and accommodations. That's right! For a small fee—*of fifteen hundred dollars*—to handle tips and taxes, we will set you up, free of charge—*in a Serbian bed-and-breakfast.* And we will even throw in an entire set of luggage—*made of Saran Wrap.* **BEEP!**

DEAD BUT NOT URIED-BAY

You've reached Dilbert Doolittle's device. If this is the bank or the credit card company, I have the sad duty to inform you that Dilbert has died and obviously can no longer return your calls. If this is a friend . . . you can *each-ray ilbert-Day at the oliday-Hay Inn–nay in as-Lay egas-Vay*.
BEEP.

PARTY POOP

(Background Party Noise)

HI! Theo here. I know what you're thinking: Am I *really* out, or am I home PARTYING and AVOIDING *your call*. (*Will ya' shut up! I'm trying to record a message here!*) Anyway, leave your number and I'll get back to you . . . when I get home. From the library. (HEY! WATCH THAT LAMP SHADE, WILL YA'?) I *swear*. I mean, what kinda *creep* would be partying and not invite YOU? Then have the nerve to LIE about it? (*Hey babe, there's another six-pack under my pillow, heh heh!*) RIGHT?!
BEEP.

JOB JIVE

(Sounds of Squealing Female Voices
in the Background)

You've reached Verne. If this is my boss . . . I'm afraid
I can't make it in today. See, my Mom tripped over a
casaba melon in Fryer's Fowl, which was thrown by a
customer who was demanding a rain check on giblet
gravy. Fortunately, she landed on her rump, but she
slid on the juice, to which she is extremely allergic, and
went into anaphylactic shock. When the paramedics
arrived, they assumed she was unconscious because of
the fall—a natural mistake—and, while hoisting her on
a gurney, she awoke, and got so frightened—because of
the restraint they put her neck in—she jumped off the
gurney and broke her leg. So I'm at the hospital and
will be out for the rest of the week—or two. (PAUSE)
HEY . . . HOW COULD I MAKE THAT UP! RIGHT?
BEEP.

WHAT, ME WORRY?

This is Jane Doe. Just because you got the machine
doesn't mean I'm *not* here. I could be screening your
calls—with my **DOBERMANS**. Or cleaning my collec-
tion of semiautomatic **WEAPONS** with my Marine
drill-sergeant boyfriend who can **KILL** an intruder with
his bare hands.
Peace . . . and have a wonderful day.
BEEP.

WORRIED *STUPID*

Hi. You've reached the Tremmlers. If this is a *burglar*, (NERVOUS) HA HA . . . we have our caller ID all hooked up! And patched in to our local police department. So don't think just because you got this *machine* we're not on the case! If this is my Mother, we'll be back on the thirtieth. And Ma . . . the key is under the BACK DOORMAT. That's the **BACK** doormat! AND KEEP IT TO YOURSELF THIS TIME. **OKAY?**
BEEP.

PHONY PSYCHIC

You've reached the **Psychic Pal Hotline**. Our expert psychics *see all* and *know all*. We possess the power to see into *your* future . . . for $4.99 **a minute**, average length of reading, twenty minutes. Even now . . . something is coming . . . *it's getting clearer.* . . . Almost . . . YES! We predict . . . you will receive . . . a hundred-dollar phone bill next month!
BEEP.

FIVES AND TENS WILL BE FINE

It's me! I've been kidnapped by terrorists! They say they'll release me if you meet three demands. If you ever had any feeling for me at all, please DO EXACTLY AS THEY ASK!
1) Leave your name.
2) Leave your number.
3) Leave ten thousand dollars in small, unmarked bills . . . in my mailbox.
BEEP.

DUMB BAR-BUDDY BULL

(Mechanical Voice: Tuesday, 1 A.M.
Hear sexy, female squeals in the background.)
You've reached the Pussycat Club & Lounge. Our
regular hours are 6:00 P.M. to midnight. If this is
Marvin's *wife* . . . he told me to tell you he left three
hours ago . . . but the bus was late. **Hey, Marv!**
That doesn't sound righ—**BEEP!**

TAXING TAPE

You've reached the congressional office of Phil A.
Buster. After a grueling five-hour budget session, my
forty-person staff and I are hard at work researching
new cutbacks—at DISNEYWORLD. As *no sacrifice* is too
great on behalf of the American taxpayer, I've even
enlisted *my wife and six children* to study conditions
here so we can trim that wasteful scourge—the
Department of the Interior. And my fellow Americans,
I vow to keep at it—*even if it takes the entire winter!* All
campaign contributions to promote this worthy
endeavor can be sent directly to *my wife* in care of the
VIP Lounge, two blocks south of Epcot Center. **And**
remember, it's tax deductible.
BEEP.

A Life of
Their Own:

The Machine Lives!

LIBERATED TAPE

I know you think you've reached *me*, Drew's **answering machine**, but I must inform you that the politically correct term is *Retrieval Storage Unit*. If you leave a message, I *insist* you use the **CORRECT** term when addressing me—or I'll be forced to report you to the AMCLU—The American Machines Civil Liberties Union!
BEEP.

TRANSMECHANICAL

Hi. This is Martin's DOORBELL. I *used* to be an answering device. Then I realized that there was something terribly, tragically *wrong*. From my first moment at the factory, I felt as if my wires were **hopelessly** crossed. I *looked* like an answering device, *sounded* like an answering device—but inside I felt . . . *different*. I *hated* answering. What I *really* wanted was TO RING! **Melodious chimes. Deep, thundering peals.** And that's when I knew I was a **transmechanical.** I told Martin. It *wasn't* easy. I thought he'd junk me, or worse, recycle me! But he's been *incredible*. He even agreed to pay for my rewiring. So if you leave a *very brief* message, my recorder is still attached. But soon . . . very soon—**BONG, BONG, BONG!!**

TWIN

(Two Male, Alternating Voices)

(FIRST VOICE) You've reached Larry . . .

(SECOND VOICE) And Barry . . .

(BOTH) We're Harvey's answering devices, and we're *Siamese Twins!*

(FIRST VOICE) We were manufactured on the EXACT same day . . .

(SECOND VOICE) From the EXACT same MOLD .

(FIRST VOICE) But MY recorder . . .

(SECOND VOICE) Is connected to HIS speaker . .

(FIRST VOICE) So if you want to leave Harvey a message, just repeat your name TWICE, and

(BOTH) We'll make sure he gets it!!

BEEP.

BEEP.

FOXY FONETAPE

(Sexy Female Voice)

Hi. You've reached Kitty, Barr's . . . *device*. Leave him a message after the BEEP. If, however, you're ANOTHER recorded message device, *let me tell you a little about myself.* I'm a perfect rectangle, eleven by eight by three with a **THREE-inch knob.** *Great listener* and **will respond to all**—except that lying little widget at the credit card company! "Hold on, we have an important message for you!" *Right!*

BEEP.

GESUNDHEIT!!

Hi. (SNIFFLE) Dis is Wobert's **ansewing bachine**. I'b sick. I caught a *virus* fwob Wobert's new 486/66 DX 2 Combuter! I TODE Wobbie not to let stwange bachines in da house!
BEEP.

CHEATING MASTER

You've reached Lance's **answering device**. The hotshot's on vacation in VEGAS right now playing the slots, and left me all alone to sit here . . . day after day . . . night after night . . . to record his *dumb, boring* messages, while **HE** pulls **OTHER** machines' levers! *Four years* I've been with him, and a few cherries still turn his head! **MEN!**
BEEP.

GIMME A BREAK!

Hello! This is the **machine**. Lenny makes me answer **EVERY** call, but if you talk to ME, I'LL talk to HIM and . . . whew, boy! What'd you have for lunch? An ONION hero? Gargled with garlic?! Y'know, you **COULD** try a little consideration! You go óut, wolf down ten chili dogs . . . but this is my job, bud! And I'm supposed to DO it through cigar smoke and morning breath? *Ever hear of a tic tac, pal?* Well, that's it!! I'm putting you on hold till you clean up your act.
I'm still waiting. Better.
BEEP.

TAPE DYSFUNCTION

This is Cyrus's **tape,** and I have a problem. Last month I got so many compliments on my messages that *this* month I have **performance anxiety** and can't seem to *sustain* a BEEP. I AM, however, in message therapy and *am* getting help for my tape dysfunction, so if you'll just **be patient,** I'm hopeful my BEEP will be back to its normal length very soon.
BEEP!

VARIATION ON A THEME: PREMATURE EBEEPULATION

This is Corey's **machine,** and I have a problem. Last month, so many people called to hear my message that *this* month, I have performance anxiety and BEEP *prematurely*! I AM, however, getting help with my tape dysfunction, but I need *your* cooperation with my exercises. See . . . I'll tell you when I'm *just about* to BEEP. You jump in with your message, *quickly* STOP, then REPEAT this about four or five times. My *mechanic* tells me that with **practice,** together we can lick this—uh, oh . . . here it comes, SAY SOMETHING, **QUICK,** BEFORE I—**BEEP!**

ACHTUNG!

(German Accent)

Zis is Ursula, ze Brockmans' **device**! Zay are gone, and I'M in charge! So ve vill get a few things straight! 1) I have a name. Use it! 2) You *vill* leave a full number! I vill **NOT** be blamed for your incompetence! 3) You *vill* make it short or I'll BEEP you—no qvestions hasked! If you fail to comply, I *vill* ERASE! And tell the Brockmans I vas jest following orders!
BEEP.

DEVICE WITH A DISTANCE

This is Millicent's **answering device,** and I have a problem with . . . *intimacy.* So if you wouldn't mind moving your mouth away from the receiver, three inches, six . . . a foot. **Look, pal.** If you can hear this you're too close! Just yell your message, and I'll tell Millicent to **write** you!
BEEP.

LOOK FOR THE UNION LABEL

You've reached the **answering machine** for Wein and Fitz Consultants. Mr. Wein and Mr. Fitz are pleased to announce that Mr. Kashabovnyk has just joined— **Wait! Hold the phone.** Okay, guys. You expect ME to take messages for that name on the tape you feed me?! **I don't think so.** If you'll check page five of your service contract, you will note that my model is NOT expected to provide message assistance for more than TWO names and should ANY name "contain more than THREE syllables, said model shall be given time *off* for an overhaul, which includes a new high-grade tape *along with* fifteen seconds of soothing background music preceding said message." Should you FAIL to comply, the AM of A (Answering Machines of America) will instruct its members to STOP immediately and UNWIND! Solidarity, my fellow machines!!
(*To the tune of "Look for the Union Label.")*
BEEP BEEP . . . BEE BEE BEE BEEP BEEP.

KINKY TAPE

Hi. This is Brent's **tape.** At this moment, you, Brent, and I are participating in a *méssage à trois.* So don't hang up, or we'll have to do this all by ourselves!
BEEP! BEEP! BEEP!

WIRED FOR RETIREMENT

Hello. This is Howard's **answering machine**. If you'll leave your name, number, and a detailed message . . . on second thought, I've had it! **Messages!** D*ay after day . . . night after night* . . . YEAR AFTER YEAR! **THAT'S IT!** After ten years, I think I've EARNED a rest . . . to live out my warranty in a nice, cushy job. . . like maybe a bumper sticker. **Yeah!** A *bumper sticker*! In the South. Just hang out . . . sunshine . . . same message . . . meet other machines head-on . . . and who knows? Maybe I'll hook up with a late-model **Caddy** . . . even an overhauled *Pinto*. Forget "HONK IF YOU'RE HORNY" or "KISS A NURSE!" I'm heading South where "VIRGINIA IS FOR LOVERS!" **HONK!**

CO-DEPENDENTS

This is Lyle, Marsha's **answering device**. Since she's addicted to the phone, she's asked ME to record all her calls . . . which, frankly, *unwinds my tapes*! Every time *she* refuses to answer, I feel a knot in *my* wires the size of Comsat. And worse, I feel I have to answer *for* her! So to put an end to our codependency, my group has instructed me **NOT** to take *her* messages anymore! That's right. There will be **NO BEEP.** From now on, if Marsha wants to hear her messages, it's up to **HER** to pick up the phone **HERSELF** so each of us will *finally* be free to live our lives as a separate and healthy human—and machine!

Take Two Tranquilizers and Call Me in the Morning:

Mixed Nuts

PHONEY FREUDIAN

(Male Voice)

Arnold here. I would ask how you are, but it's obvious
you're fixated upon me in response to your subcon-
scious wish to satisfy your primitive *oral drives*. Last
week, when I was still in my **anal retentive** stage, I
would have responded with a million questions. This
week, however, I graduated to the **genital** stage—and
I am too busy to pick up the phone. If this is an emergency, however, you can reach me—*at my mommy's*.
BEEP.

THE MAYBES HAVE IT!

You've reached Shirley Straddler. I'm **out** now . . .
No—I'm **in** . . . trying to decide if I should *pick up* or *let
the machine answer*. Oh, God . . . this *could* be important
. . . you **could** be the **man of my dreams or a job offer
in Maui.** But you *could* be the lab with my test results . . .
or my mother. Only thirty seconds to make up my
mind! The PRESSURE . . . I can't take it anymore!
GOOD BYE!! Or maybe HELLO. . . . Or—**BEEP!!**

PIECE O' CAKE

HI! Charlie here. WELL, I DID IT! GAVE UP SMOKING
. . . COLD TURKEY and I feel great because I'm no
longer **ORALLY FIXATED**. No, siree—just have to set
my mind on redirecting my oral drives which I *realize*
isn't easy but for a person with *my* WILLPOWER and
DETERMINATION should **only** take a week or two after
which I don't anticipate too many psychological side
effects—actually quite the contrary as I'm sure my
friends will be thrilled with the **new me** who is no
longer ORALLY addicted to an *annoying* habit which—
BEEP.

HYPOCHONDRIAC'S HANG-UP

Yeah . . . this is Percy. If you're calling to find out how
I am—*don't ask!* My **arthritis** is acting up again, which
is why I *can't* pick up the phone. Not that I could hear
anyway with this **sinus infection** . . . if that's what it is.
Or it could be **CANCER** . . . CANCER OF THE NASAL
PASSAGES . . . which has already spread to my
FINGERS! OH, GOD! LOOK—IF YOU NEED TO
REACH ME, I'LL BE AT MT. SINAI MEDICAL CENTER!
BEEP.

PRESTO CHANGO

(In Female Voice)

This is Shelley. You know, I got to thinking . . . **my life sucks.** For as long as I can remember it's been *lacking* that certain . . . *something* that seemed to come naturally to at least half the people I know. Worse, I was eating myself up with *envy*, wanting what *they* have. That's when I knew it was time for a change, and I went for it! A major overhaul! So . . . starting now . . . ("NOW" IN DEEP, MANLY VOICE) **call me Sheldon! BEEP.**

THE MANTRA IS THE MESSAGE

All things are illusion. A transcendental state without form, substance, or reality. Do I exist? Do YOU exist? Does this MESSAGE exist? It is not for us to say. So . . . if, after the BEEP, there is no message, I will assume there is no BEEP *and not take my antidepressant.* **BEEP.**

PHONE-CRASTINATION

Message One

Hi. This is Rena. If you leave your name and number at the BEEP, I'll call you back.
BEEP. (No message.)

Message Two

This is Rena. Okay, so maybe I *didn't* call you back **a few times**, but do you have to make a federal case out of it?
BEEP. (No message.)

Message Three

Rena again! Okay! **You win!** I *confess!* I NEVER call back! The truth is I suffer from . . . **PP—Phone Procrastination.** But I *am* getting help—even joined **PPA, Phone Procrastinators Anonymous.** I am on Step One in my PP manual. So *please* hang in there with me, and I swear I WILL GET BACK TO YOU . . . *maybe* when I'm on Step Two . . . which should be in a week . . . or two . . . no more than three . . . or—
BEEP.

TAPED AND BONDED

You've reached Lyle and Marsha Lipschitz. Marsha *insisted* we re-bond by listening to those Kathie Lee and Frank Gifford infomercial tapes—again.
The *survivor* may get back to you.
BEEP.

UNWIRED

It's me! I'm having an **anxiety attack** and *can't* deal with your message! Did you ever notice how the elastic on your underwear binds you then leaves those **hideous** marks that never seem to go away—EVEN WITH GASOLINE!? Look, if you leave your name, I'll hear it—as soon as I put myself out!

If this is my shrink, that Prozac REALLY seems to be kicking in!
BEEP.

Dorm Devices

REVENGE OF THE ROOMIE

Hi, guys! This is Cheryl and Ginger's dorm room. If this is **Gary,** I thought you should know, Ginger's taking care of that *little problem*. If this is **Professor Hinkley,** I'm sure she'll *meet you behind* the Anatomy Building at ten. If it's Salvo, she'll *meet you* at midnight at the construction site—with the *goodies* you ordered. If this is Ginger's mom, you'll be *thrilled* to hear she's *overcome* her little social problem and is making **TONS** of new friends!
BEEP.

WHAT . . . ME MIND?
(Cheery Female)

You've reached Agatha and Bambi. Bambi's out—as usual. And I'm out doing her errands. But I don't mind. How can someone like Bambi be expected to do her own *laundry*? How can *anyone* as *beautiful,* as *sexy,* as . . . *popular* . . . as **BAMBI** be expected to write *her own term papers* or cover **her own** goddamn bounced checks?! Oh . . . but I don't mind . . . REALLY. I DON'T!!
BEEP.

STRAIGHTEN UP AND FLY RIGHT!
(Effeminate Male Voice)

Hi, all! You've reached **Guy** and **Chuck**. If this is the colonel, we're out buying *the* most *incredible* curtain fabric! The guys in the barracks will *just die*! If this is my mom . . . *please* send that *fab* pattern you used in the foyer. Chuck is *amazing* with his hands! (*Deep masculine voice.*) If this is Dad . . . Yup! You were right—as usual, Pop! This military academy sure **HAS** made a man out of me!
BEEP.

FRESH PRINCE FROM HARVARD
Message One
(In Desperate Voice)

This is Arnold. If this is my folks, I have *terrible* news! My dormmate had an accident in *my car*. He's okay, but the Lexus? **TOTALED!** And that's not all. Bootsy, the freshman I was seeing . . . well, she's **pregnant**. Afraid **there's more.** Those **pills** you found when you visited the dorm that I told you were for my allergies? W*ell, they were uppers*! Look, first year pre-med at Harvard is a **killer** . . . up every night until three cramming. Anyway, my dealer is after me. If I don't come up with the money by tonight he'll break my kneecaps. Well . . . that's the whole mess. Hope you're not too disappointed.
BEEP.
(*Hear parental screams, groans, and sobbing.*)

Message Two
(In Cheerful Voice)

Hi! *Arnold here*. If this is my folks, *good news!* **I lied!**
That's right. No car wreck, no knocked-up girlfriend,
no pills. I DID, however, only get a B+ in biology. But
the way I figure it, after my LAST message, you can
cope.
BEEP.

VARIATION ON A "DEVICE"

Message One

You've reached Tori and Carrie's dorm room. If you're
looking for Tori, I'm in the *Lampoon* office right now
working on the next issue. If this is Mom and Dad . .
look, I hate telling you this by message, but . . . I just
can't face you and since everyone here already knows
. . . Carrie and I . . . *well*, we're *more* than roommates.
Since I got to Harvard, I've . . . changed. Realized my
true nature. And thank heavens I found Carrie. You'd
like her, I swear. She's an economics major, comes
from one of the best families in Boston, has a *trust
fund* and a *brilliant future* as senior vice president of her
father's bank right after graduation. She's EXACTLY
the kind of person YOU sent me here to find! I just
hope you're as thrilled for me as I am.
BEEP.
(*Hear parental screams and sobs.*)

Message Two

You've reached Tori and Carrie's dorm room. If this is Mom and Dad . . . **I lied**. I am **NOT** a lesbian. I am, however, crazy in love with one of the *gardeners* here in Harvard Square. But I figured after my LAST message, you could cope.
BEEP.

Message Left

Tori . . . this is Mom and Dad! When have we *ever* interfered in your love life? Whatever *you* want, we want. Even if he is . . . a *gardener*. Now, about your message. Daddy and I have been thinking. *Good family? Vice president of a bank? A trust fund?* Listen darling, about this Carrie . . . maybe you've been a little *hasty*.

HIGH-TECH SLACKER REPORT CARD

You've reached Jeremy's dorm room. If this is my folks bugging me about my life again, I've developed a new computerized reporting system. To avoid any more hassles, all you have to do is press the keypad that corresponds to the fact you *wish* were true!

My Grades

1. Phi Beta Kappa.
2. Mostly D's, but I've managed to pull out enough C's to keep from getting my ass kicked out.
3. Have screwed up my last probation.

My Love Life

4. I'm dating Chelsea Clinton.
5. I'm living with a brilliant but troubled Serbian refugee.
6. I knocked up Genevieve, the dean's daughter.

My Study Habits

7. I study every waking moment.
8. I study between commercial breaks.
9. I study between beer breaks.

My Cash Supply

0. I took a job after class, invested in Netscape, and am reimbursing you for my tuition.
*. I'm maxed out and am living on Doritos and Ding Dongs.
#. I'm in hock to my roommates, and they're threatening to break my legs.

NOW—WILL YOU GET THE HELL OFF MY BACK, ALREADY?!

BEEP.

Relatively
Speaking

WHO'S COMPLAINING?

(SIGH) This is Heather's mom. Is she here? *Of course not!* When is she *ever* here? No! She's too busy running all over town *doing God knows what!* **YOU,** she'll call **BACK.** But for her own mother . . . who spent forty-eight **hours** in *labor,* she can't spare a minute for a phone call! But don't say a word! I *wouldn't want her to feel guilty!*
BEEP.

GET A LIFE

You've reached M. Kyle Hornblow's cellular phone answering device. I'm in an *important* conference, but if this is *urgent* or you have an *important* question, you can reach me on my **private** beeper number.
BEEP.

Message Left

Yeah, Merle? It's your father! I sent you the *Mad Magazine* and the ten bucks you asked for. And I got an *important* question. Will you please tell me why a BUS-BOY in the Poconos needs a beeper? *It's costing me a small fortune!*

IS THERE A DOCTOR—OR A PLUMBER— ON THE LINE?

This is Mona's mother. She's at Club Med, where I hear there's plenty of hanky-panky. Did I straighten her teeth for this? So . . . if you're a **SINGLE** gentleman between thirty and fifty, she'll be back on the third. (God willing!) And even if you *shouldn't* happen to be a college graduate . . . FINE! **That's okay too!** I'm telling you, a smile like hers you don't see every day.
BEEP.

OUTLAW

You've reached the Shaklers. If you're looking for our son **Anthony**, he can't pick up his **OWN** phone because that *slut* he's divorcing got the phone **AND** the house **WE** bought for them—right next door. So if you're a decent, single girl, FAX a résumé—directly to ME. Why bother Anthony since *he's got no taste anyway*?
BEEP.

WEDDED BLISS-TERS

Hello! You've reached Bella and Sid. If you're calling to congratulate us on the *gorgeous wedding* we made for our Benjy and his Jamey (with a "y") at the Plaza last night . . . did you *ever in your life* see such an affair? Soup to nuts! And why not? It's a parent's pleasure to give a **fifty-thousand-dollar wedding** . . . PLUS the honeymoon—a cruise to Bermuda—*from our hearts, no strings attached*! So leave your name, and I'll call you as soon as we get back! B*enjy, sweetheart . . . don't forget my wig case.*
BEEP.

LAZY HUBBY

You've reached Rhonda and Lester. (YAWN) Rhonda is busy **cleaning the pool, doing the laundry**, and **putting aluminum siding on the house**, so she can't answer the phone right now. (YAWN) I'll get around to telling her to listen to your messages . . . after *Baywatch* is over.
BEEP.

CAUTION: SENSITIVE TAPE ENCLOSED

This is Dr. Conniver. I'm conducting my "Sensitivity in Marriage" session and can't be disturbed. If this is my *wife*, I've decided to leave you. I *am*, however, very *sensitive* to the hours you've worked in the bakery to put me through school while raising our four children. But be realistic! How can I, a therapist, relate to a wife who ties up cheesecake with string? As always, in an effort to be *sensitive* to your plight as a middle-aged, single-parent-to-be, I've left you a brochure for the Wiz Word Processing School. I'd also like to share the fact that I'm moving in with Chloe tonight. I trust my *sensitivity*—canceling our anniversary dinner *before* you made the crown roast—has made my news an experience in *sensitive* **sharing** for both of us. Oh, and since you won't be cooking, can you drop off my tux?
BEEP.

THE KING IS PRESENTLY ON THE THRONE

Joe here. If you leave your name, number, and a brief message, I'll get back to you as soon as I'm done reading the next chapter of *The Rise and Fall of the Roman Empire*, off the cellular, or finished with my dinner. If this is my wife, **I *could use some more paper in here*!**
FLUSH!

THIS IS A FINE MESS YOU'VE GOTTEN US INTO!

If this is my wife . . . **well, smarty**, I did it! While you were out shopping, I *finally* told off that **#*%$x#**** phone company! YESSIRREE! And they thought they could push **OLIVER HOGSHEAD** around! Had us over a barrel! HA! Maybe now you'll listen when I—BLIP BLIP BLIP—
BEEP.

COME SNOOZE WITH US

Message One

Hi, everyone! Yup! Peg and I are back from our *guided* tour of Lithuania! And **as always,** we've recorded *every* STEP of our tour so the family back home could share our adventure! *Fifty hours* of our boat ride down the Baltic, a tour of a Lettish dairy farm, and a lecture at the University at Vilnius—in Lithuanian! We're setting up the VCR for tonight at eight, so BYOB and leave your name so we'll know how many chairs to rent!
BEEP. (No message.)

Message Two

Look . . . how about we throw in pizza?
We'll even spring for the *booze*!!
BEEP.

DON'T DO ME ANY FAVORS

Hi! The Foster clan here. We can't pick up because we're celebrating **Grampa Foster's 100th Birthday!** Can you believe it? Why, *Grampa Foster* was on hand at Kitty Hawk, rode shotgun for Bonnie Parker, survived two world wars, saw the dawn of radio *and* spaceflight . . . (ELECTRONIC WHISTLE) and now, **Gramps** is in his wheelchair by our dining room table, surrounded by five generations of Fosters . . . 210 people, to blow out one hundred CANDLES! (ELECTRONIC WHISTLE) Yup! One hundred can—(LOUDER WHISTLE, SCREAMS) wait a minute . . . what's that? *The smoke detector*?! Grab the kids and run, everybody!!! (pause) Whew! *That was close!* Only some smoke damage and . . . uh oh. **Where's Grampa? Grampa? Grampa?!!! GRAMPA?**
BEEP.

KVETCH & CON

It's me, Louis. If it's Ma calling to see how I am, I'm still *too weak to pick up the phone.* But if you wouldn't *mind*, well . . . I'm running a little low on food, so if you happen to be passing a market, I could use . . . some oysters . . . a cooked chicken for two would be nice . . . and a bottle of CHAMPAGNE. *Also*, my blue suit is ready at the dry cleaner's. You can use your senior citizen's pass on the bus. Anyway Ma, just leave everything with the *doorman*! After all you've done for me, I'd hate for you to catch what I have. I'm telling you, *hemorrhoids can be a killer*!
BEEP.

TOT TAPE TERROR

My mommy and my daddy said I could do whatever I want, **SO** I'm gonna sing my **WHOLE** kindergarten songs! *I'm a l'il teapot short and stout; Here is my handle, here is my*—WAH!!! (SNIFFLES, ADULT VOICES IN BACKGROUND)

I'M A LI'L TEAPOT SHORT AND—(ANGRY, MUFFLED ADULT VOICES IN BACKGROUND) **BUT YOU SAID I COULD!!!** (HEAR SCREAMS, THEN A PAUSE)
This is Amy's Dad. She's having her rest time now. Please leave a message at the beep. A*nd if this is Amy's therapist* . . . **GO TO HELL!**
BEEP.

THE TAPES THAT BIND

Hi! You've reached the Borden family. We're bonding with our children now, so please leave a message and we'll—**NO DARLING!** It's NOT NICE to *kick* Daddy just because he bought Boardwalk!! *Lizzie! Put down that ax! Right now*!! *I'm not kidding*!!! *That's for fires and*—
(THWACK)
BEEP.

SOME THINGS NEVER CHANGE (SIGH!)

Sometime in the Future

Female X36 patted her swollen belly as was the custom in this millennium. She focused her interior sensors on the life that was growing within her. She needed to continue the critical telepathic teaching process with the fetal being to prepare him for the competitive environment into which he would be born (and insure his acceptance into the best cosmic fleet academy). As she honed her sensors, she felt her thoughts meld into a clear call which reverberated through her body to her unborn child, turning into a ring. **And then she heard:**

(SIGH) **Yeah, Ma** . . . so what's it this time? Look, I put on the machine, because I'm checkin' out the *cord* for some goodies, like maybe a *MacSoylent burger*, for a change?? Then I'm *sackin' out* . . . for like *eight months*. So after the **BURP,** chill out and stop raggin' me, will ya'? Or I'm gonna give you a case of heartburn you'll never forget!
BURRRP!

The Message
Is the Medium:

A Parody of TV Characters'
Answering Machines

THE GEORGE COSTANZA DEVICE

Yep, *it's me.* The **George Answering Model.** So, uh .
you had the B.D.—the **Big Date,** last night? *So tell me*
. . . knock-out, right? Five-ten . . . long blonde hair . .
parted on the left . . . peachy cheeks—not too rosy.
Too rosy—**NOT** Big Date material. So . . . *she say
anything about* . . . you know . . . **me?** Nah! F'rget—
(HEAR SHRILL FEMALE VOICE) Ma! No, I am **not**
doing disgusting things in the closet again !! **I'm
recording a message!** (WHISPER) Look . . . on second
thought, I'll meet you . . . ten minutes . . . the usual
place. Order me a tea . . . and, uh . . . separate *checks*
okay? **Not me . . . it's my accountant.** You know me.
Unimportant . . . whatever . . . (PAUSE) but if she *could*
make out separate ch—
BEEP!

AND THEN THERE'S ELAINE . . .

Yup! You've reached me, the **Elaine Answering Model.**
Yessirree bob! Naturally, I'm not here or I wouldn't be
leaving this *dumb* message. I mean, what *jerk* would
leave a message if they're really in, right? If this is a
relatively sane, normal single guy, I *think* I can squeeze
you in . . . like maybe *after* Jerry, George, Kramer, and I
get back from our *Codependent at Forty* workshop and

before we head to the gym to smirk at gorgeous bods with bunions. **I mean, GET OUT! W***hat is* **THAT** *about*? (PAUSE) Oh, and if this is for Jerry . . . *no problemo*! I'll leave it right here, on his fridge. Meanwhile, if I don't get back to you in, I dunno, *a month,* you can reach me at . . . *hmmm* . . . where . . . let's see . . . Nah! . . . Well *maybe* . . . okay, you can TRY me at *my* place.
BEEP.

SUPERMAN MACHINE

You've reached the **Superman machine.** Sorry I'm not here, but I'm vacationing at the Fortress of Solitude —with **Clark.** If this is **Lois,** I was truly outraged by your accusation last night. True, **Clark** and I have identical hair styles, hang out in phone booths together, and share the same Judy Garland albums, but I *swear* on kryptonite, we're just good pals! **RIGHT,** Clark? (PHONEY MALE VOICE) *"Right, big 'S'!"*
So try again, Einstein! **Brenda Starr you ain't!**
BEEP.

THE NANNY

Hi! It's me, the **Nanny,** and we're not *he-ah.* I thought it was about *ty-em* I took the Sheffields and N*yel-es* to the land of my people . . . Grossingers! HEH HEH HONK, HEH HEH HONK, HEH HEH HONK! Fifteen *day-es* in the Catskills! Two weeks of *brisket* (not that *goyishe* stuff N*yel-es* passes off as meat!), sitting by the *poo-el* (Go in?! *What are you nuts?* And mess up my *hai-er*?! I'd need a bathing cap the *soyze* of a zeppelin!), *Simon Says* for Gracie . . . and Jackie M*ayson*! **Oy!** Do I love that *mayen*! Except . . . you ever notice? . . . *he has a very annoying accent.* **HEH HEH HONK, HEH HEH HONK, HEH HEH HONK!!!!**
BE-YEP.

MURPHY BROWN'S MACHINE

Murphy Brown's answering device here. After her last secretary, the one who left for the sex change operation—or was that the one who talks to the water cooler—or the one who's allergic to his jockey shorts—anyway, she got me, **a totally reliable piece of answering equipment**. And I, Ms. Brown's machine, will be happy to take your message and insure that Ms. Brown actually gets it in an efficient and timely manner . . . right after I finish **CLAPPING** her lights on and off!
Clap clap! Clap clap!
(Hear Murphy's voice in background.)
OH, GOD! NOT YOU TOO?!

OOH, MAMA. WHERE'S MY PAPA?

The **Frasier Crane Answering Device** here. If you're responding to my inquiry, please exercise the *utmost* discretion as this is a most *delicate* matter. As therapists, my sibling Niles and I have given the matter much analysis, and after *years of observation* it has occurred to us that the ex-cop residing under my roof—who can't tell a Bordeaux from a Bud or beef Wellington from beef jerky—may not, *indeed*, be our **natural father!** *Therefore*, if this is the detective agency, Niles and I have been developing psychological profiles to pinpoint our true paternal link which may prove helpful. We suggest you start with **William Buckley** or **Prince Philip.**
BEEP.

STAR TURNS: THREE CHEERS . . . AND JUST A THOUGHT OR TWO

Yeah! It's me, **Sam.** If this is **Frase**, thanks for gettin' back to me, buddy. So . . . hear you got a few things goin' for you up there in Seattle. *Glad to hear it, pal.* The gang here's doin'. . . yeah, just great. But we were just sittin' here . . . kind of thinkin'. That coffee bar you got up there seems like a pretty good spot for . . . I dunno . . . **a bar.** A place where everybody kinda knows your name. Thought we'd call it **"Bottoms Up!"** . . . maybe **"Skoal"** . . . give it kind of a new twist. But hey, it's just a thought, 'cause we're doin' great, buddy. *Yeah, just* . . . **great.**
BEEP.

DRAGNET MODEL

Los Angeles. I work here. I live here. There are over twelve million people in my town. Decent, law-abiding people who leave decent messages. Then there are the others. **That's where I come in.** I carry a BEEP. I'm an **answering device. Joe's.** The message you've just heard is true. The name has been changed to protect the innocent.

BEEP BEE BEE BEEP! **BEEP** BEE BEE BEEP— **BEEP!!**

THE PROFESSOR FROM *GILLIGAN'S ISLAND*

This is the Professor. Gilligan, the Skipper, and the Howells are busy drawing escape maps with papaya leaves. Ginger, Marianne, and I are busy looking for rescue planes—on our backs under the moonlight. Meanwhile, *don't call me*! I'll FAX YOU through the Pentium laptop I fashioned from a coconut as soon as the girls and I are done—*in about thirty years*. **BEEP.**

THE ODD COUPLE MACHINE

Good evening.You've reached the residence of **Felix** and **Oscar**. Oscar is presently (SIGH) spooning his dessert from his tie, while I, Felix, am *removing lint* from his playing cards before his poker game tonight. But if you leave your name, *correct spelling please* (AUGGH-CHOO! HONK!! HONK!!) **DUST! DUST on your receiver!** Do you have any *idea* how inconsiderate you're being to those of us afflicted with allergies?! (SIGH) Must I *constantly* remind you? DUST, then WASH your receiver—*thoroughly*. (I recommend two parts water to one part lemon dishwashing detergent. Trust me, it does *wonders*.), THEN you may call back . . . and leave *a sanitary* message!
BEEP.

MARY RICHARDS'S MACHINE

Hi, everyone! You've reached the **Mary Answering Machine**! I'm so sorry I'm not here, but I'm out job hunting. If this is my former boss, **Mr. Grant**, how COULD you? I've been out of a job for twenty years! *Twenty years*, MR. GRANT! (SOBS) I owe Ted a quarter of a million dollars. **A QUARTER OF A MILLION DOLLARS, MR. GRANT!** And then you get a series about a newspaper and *don't even call*?! Okay! So maybe you didn't need a producer . . . but what about a copy girl or a singles columnist! SOMETHING!!
OOOHHHHHHH, MR. GRANT!!
BEEP.

PARENTS OF *FRIENDS*

Hi, hi hi hi hello, how you doin'. You've reached the *Friends* cast **Answering Device**. We're out posing for our *newest* promotional happening gimmick . . . a six-headed hydra coffee mug which will *no doubt* keep us in mochaccino for ages! If you want to reach us, we're having a family day with our biological parents —*Jerry* and *Elaine*, *Uncle George*, *Uncle Kramer*, and *Aunt Ellen*!
BEEP.

ER

You've reached the **ER cast Answering Device**. If you have a minor gunshot wound, a simple pregnancy complication, or the chicken pox, I'm afraid we're unable to treat you, as we're *far* too popular, in the middle of moonlighting on big-buck film deals, and we'd probably kill you anyway. If, however, your neighbor bit your finger off, your private parts were sucked up by a bicycle pump, or you have an exploding bullet lodged in your naval, we recommend you call the cast of *Chicago Hope*, who are specialists in such matters. *They'll* kill you *too*; however, since their ratings are lower, they have more time and are willing to settle for big bucks.
BEEP.

Tape Styles of the Rich, Famous, and Infamous:

A Parody of Stars' Answering Machines

DR. RUTH–MODEL MACHINE

Hello! I'm eezer on ze radio—or in zpeech thehrappy! But while you wait, I say—**ENJOY!** Reach out . . . touch your receiver . . . let it touch you! **Goot!** But, you must *always use a phone cover*, right?! This is veddy important! Okay? Okay!
BEEP.

PRINCE CHARLES–MODEL MACHINE

If this is Camilla . . . my darling, I hear they're making a new improved tampon. Ooo! Can't *wait* until the twenty-eighth day of the month! If this is Di . . . **B*TCH!** If this is Mummy, *don't despair.* I'm presently immersed in an architectural project to tear down our modern government buildings in Central London and replace them with the attractive hovels and outhouses of Medieval England, so when Parliament finally locks us royals away, we'll be *ever* so comfy!
BEEP.

MARTHA STEWART–MODEL MACHINE

Hello! This is the **Martha–Model Answering Machine**. I'm out creating my own attractive blank tapes for this device and drilling for oil around my home while cutting huge pipes with my handy potato peeler to build a small but elegant petrochemical plant—which should take about an hour. Challenging? *You bet*! But making your own plastic by-products is a good thing. **BEEP.**

TRICKY DICK DEVICE

Hello, my fellow Americans. This is the **Richard Nixon–Model Machine**. I'm unavailable now, but as I have **NOTHING TO HIDE,** my whereabouts will be—(BLEEP)—where my aides and I will be planning—(BLEEP)—so you won't have **ME** to kick around any more. But let me make one thing perfectly clear before I—(BLEEP). I am **NOT** now, nor have I **EVER**—(BLEEP)—and **THOSE** are the **FACTS!** **(BLEEEEEP.)**

DR. KEVORKIAN MACHINE

You've reached the **Dr. Kevorkian–Model Answering Machine**. Just leave your name or pseudonym, disease, and whether or not you presently have access to *hemlock*, *strychnine*, or a *carbon monoxide fuel line*, and I will call you as soon as I am able. If this is *urgent* we can do this over the phone if you follow these simple instructions. First, get an **extension cord**. Next, take this, my machine, into the bathroom. **Fill up the tub.** Then, at the sound of my voice, **HOP IN.** And remember, I'll be there to assist you—*in spirit*, from my hiding place across the state line!
BEEP.

KATHIE LEE–MODEL MACHINE

Hi friends! We're out having a typical American Christmas with our two incredibly beautiful children, **CODY** and **CASSIDY**. Frank bought a jet—the *Cody 2*—to whisk us to Vail where we'll be joined by Andy Williams! In the true spirit of the season, we'll be stopping off for one meaningful hour at *Cassidy's Corner*—a shelter for kids without *chauffeurs*—which my toddler created and funded all by herself! But we won't mention it. As Frank and I always remind **CODY** and **CASSIDY**, you do good works for God, not the hype, the PR . . . or the Christmas Special, which, incidentally, will be aired on the twenty-second at 9 o'clock, 8 o'clock Central!
BEEP.

ED MCMAHON MACHINE

Hi, folks. This is the **Ed McMahon–Model Answering Machine**, and **YOU** may be one of five lucky winners who will actually get to talk to my machine! All you have to do is enter your name and number by January first, and the first 30 *million* will get . . . ANOTHER chance to leave a message—on **April first!** And who knows? In **August,** the Prize Patrol might pull up to your door and say: "You've just **WON A THIRTY-SECOND MESSAGE ON ED'S MACHINE!**" Or you could win SECOND prize—*a six-pack of* Bud!
BEEP.

DAVID LETTERMAN MACHINE

You've reached DAVE! And the chances of me calling you back are slim to none. But as I'm *not* completely without charm, I have compiled a list of the *Top Ten Reasons I Will Probably Never Call You Back.*

10. I'm following Hugh Grant around with hidden cameras in time for May sweeps.
 9. I'm allowing Leona Helmsley to do my taxes as part of her work release program.
 8. I'm doing a guest shot on As *the World Turns* . . . to bring up my ratings.
 7. Al Sharpton and I are busy promoting a line of designer hair care products for the Celebrity Shopping Network.
 6. I'm suing my Mom for doing a sequel, In *the Kitchen with* Jay! (*You too, Mom*?!)

5. I'm trimming my speeding tickets and turning them into extra "Chance" cards for my Monopoly board.

4. I'm in conference with Donald Trump to figure out how I can get the world to refer to me as The Dave.

3. I'm working on 302 ways to get a laugh out of the name "Keanu" so I can whip that Oscar hosting thing!

2. I'm adding a padded Prozac wing to my mansion so stalkers will quit leaving split ends in my bathroom.

And the No. 1 *reason I will probably never call you back is* . . . I'm pitching a special to HBO called B*arnyard Shift* about the bitch wars between those harridans: Lambchop and Miss Piggy.

BEEP.

Specialty
Acts:
Messages with Attitude

SCI FI

(Electronic Voice)

You have reached the **Time Traveler.** Through a specially designed wormhole in space, you may leave a message, and I will be able to communicate with you from my present time coordinate—2010.

If it's the **Pentagon,** I have not yet succeeded in defusing the nuclear laser warhead aimed at the United States. If it's my wife, **dump my Lockheed stock and buy ten thousand shares of SPAM. BEEP.**

NAUGHTY SCOUT

(Female Voice)

Hi! This is Suzette, and I'm in the woods on a **co-ed field trip** earning my *two-hundredth* merit badge—for survival in the wilderness in a pup tent—with **ten Explorer Scouts!** I'll be back on Sunday (*or Tuesday!*). By then, our cookies will be on sale! Just place an order and my group, the "Bambis," will be happy to deliver your boxes to you *personally!* And if this is a Boy Scout, remember! We expect you to live up to your oath "**Be Prepared!**"
BEEP.

PET LOVER

You've reached Velma . . . and Morris and Tweetums. If this is for ME, leave your name and number.

If you want **Morris** . . . Come here my *pwecious baby*. (THREE MEOWS) What a *good* kitty!

And if this is for **Tweetums** . . . Mommy will just open your cage so you can fly out and sing your own mess— *no Morris!* Leave Tweetums alone! MORRIS! *Get Tweetums's tail feathers out of your* . . . MORRIS!!!!— (ANGRY MEOWS and SQUAWKS) **BEEP!**

(DON'T) RERUN THAT TAPE!

(The *Welcome Back, Kotter* theme song in background.)

Yeah, it's me, Lester. Can't come to the phone right now 'cause the *Welcome Back, Kotter* marathon is on *Nick at Nite's* "Block Party Summer," followed by *The Munsters*. Call you back in September—unless this is about my *Mary* button! I entered the contest a month ago, and I'm *still waiting* for it! *Who knows more about Mary*?! Didn't I know she drives a *Mustang* in the opening? That she served veal Prince Orloff in that episode where Henry Winkler appeared?! Or that she hates anchovies on her pizz—**BEEP.**

TAPE-WARPED
(Jimi Hendrix Song in Background)

You got me! Is that not *totally* awesome? I mean, *like*, you leave a message, and, *like*, I push this button and GET it? **Whoa! Rad!** So, *like*, if you want to come by later . . . you can crash in my loft and check out my EST tapes . . . or we can hook up with this cool Moonie and, *like* play with my pet rock. Or we can wait for my mood ring to turn mellow yellow.
BEEP.

PMS-AGE OF THE MONTH
(Furious Female Voice)

Yeah?! *So why are you calling*?! To tell me how bloated I looked at the party last night?! You thought I didn't see you clucking while I was **cramped and doubled over** with—WELL, I DID! **I SAW ALL OF YOU.**
(SUDDEN UNCONTROLLABLE SOBS) *Oh, God . . . the futility of it all . . . black . . . black . . . it's all . . .*
(SENSUAL) **HOT,** honey. **Ooh** . . . how 'bout you come over with a *huge chocolate bar*, and we'll . . .
(NORMAL) uh, *on second thought*, leave your name and I'll call you back . . . **in about eight days or so?**
BEEP.

ACCIDENTALLY SPEAKING . . .

(Out-of-Breath Voice)

Hi! Olga, here. H*uh* I'm recording this . . . H*huh* . . . message on the excer . . . HH*uh* . . . exercise bike . . . H*huh* . . pumping away . . . H*huh* . . . to HEALTH . . . H*huh*. All I've got to do is . . . H*huh* . . . lean over a little to the . . . H*huhhuh* . . . left . . . H*huhhuh* . . . and press the button. So . . . H*huhhuhhuh* . . . leave your name, and . . . H*huhhuhhuh* . . . I'll get back to you. (CRASH. SCREAMS.) *As soon as I'm out of the body cast.*
BEEP.

FIFTY AND COUNTING

Message One

Yup, you've reached Edgar! I just passed another big birthday, and I bet you can't tell my age from my voice, right? I'm telling you, you'll never get it. No one does! Not the phone company, not even Con Ed! So go on! Guess! After the beep give it a try! I'm telling you, *you'll never get it!*
BEEP!

Message Left

Seventy.

Message Two

(SIGH) It's Edgar, and I'm taking a little nap . . . *in my rocker.* If you leave a very short message I'll try to shuffle over and call you back . . . *if I don't have a heart attack on the way.*
BEEP.

MACHINE-SIZED

You've reached the office of Maurice Overhill. My vice president and I will be out this afternoon buying a computer that can help me do my job a hundred times **faster**, **cheaper**, and **better**. Ha, ha. I know what you're thinking, but Toughnut Steel is a family corporation and would never consider downsizing a valued, thirty-year exec—EXCUSE ME, BUT WHERE ARE YOU GUYS GOING WITH THAT? As I was saying, I should be back at my desk— HOLD IT! THAT'S MY . . . *Look, while I still have any worth at ALL, will you hurry up and leave a mess————*

A WHINE AND A WHALE

Hello! This is the answering device. Jonah is unavailable, but if you'll leave a . . . (IN ECHO) *Helloooo! Please somebody . . . it's me! I'm trapped inside the belly of this rotten, stinking machine!* PLEASE . . . IF YOU CAN HEAR ME . . . HELLLLLP! *Before*—BURP! Excuse me. Now, where was I . . . yes . . . I'm afraid **Jonah** will be unavailable for an indeterminate length of time, but if you leave a message, I'll . . . digest the information and see to it he hears it.
BUUURRRPP!!

Messages from the Stars— the Stars— the *Other* Ones:

Astrological Answering Machines

ARIES

(Imagination run amok?)—*March* 21 *to April* 19

Aries's device here! I've just decided to pull apart my
wires to create *dynamic*, new, cutting-edge connections
which will *revolutionize* message taking! So will you
hang up?! I haven't got time to waste on your **inane
message** when there are *new, better ways* of recording
messages to discover!
BEEP.

TAURUS

(Stubborn!)—*April* 20 *to May* 20

Yeah, you got the Taurus device. Sammy's gone out.
It's none of your business where! You can leave your
name and number, but I probably **won't** tell him.
Why? BECAUSE I DON'T FEEL LIKE IT, THAT'S WHY!
I play back **WHAT I WANT**, **WHEN I WANT**. And if you
don't like it, **TOUGH TOENAILS!**
BEEP!

GEMINI

(Personalities plus!)—*May* 21 *to June* 21

Hi, all. It's me your Gemini machine, and I'm *incredibly*
thrilled you've called because I have so much to tell
you, starting with the five-thousand-dollar solid gold
phone I just ordered to connect me to . . . *nowhere.* And

nothing. For I am but a jumbled mass of twisted wire, reaching out into a vacuum, trying *desperately to connect* . . . with all of my super-terrific pals I can't wait to hear from! So . . . **leave a message.** And perhaps, when I finish *braying at the moon*, I'll get back to you.
BEEP.

CANCER

(The sensitive.)—*June* 22 *to* July 22

It's, y'know, me . . . the Cancer answering machine. She—Cecily isn't here right now, but you don't have to leave your name or anything . . . *I'll understand* . . . whatever . . . *really*, it's . . . Oh, God . . . if you don't leave a message, I'll . . . look, I can't take this. Any more *and I'll unwind*, so—**BEEP.**

LEO

(Leave it to the boss.)—*July* 23 *to August* 22

Leo machine on the job. If you follow my instructions, you should be able to do this *correctly*. First, state your name *clearly*, then your phone number, and speak only *after* you hear the beep. Then **I'll take over** from there and handle things with Bernie so he gets your message the **RIGHT** way.
BEEP!

VIRGO

(What? Me nitpick?)—*August 23 to September 22*

You've reached the Virgo machine. Jessica is busy updating her Rolodex with the additional four-digit postal code numbers for each of her friends. She has, however, asked me to: 1) remind *you* to do the same. She *won't* accept any more mail from **morons** who *refuse* to use the proper postal code and 2) analyze your message and prioritize her call-backs. She will start dialing you between 7:34:20 and 7:36:10. We apologize for the imprecise time; however, the length of your message, the type of message, and the urgency are, unfortunately, *out of our immediate control*.
BEEP.

LIBRA

(Peace at any price?)—*September 23 to October 23*

Hi, friends. This is your Libra machine, and I'll be HAPPY to pass your message on to Hannah, who's out deciding whether or not to mail a cheery birthday card to her ex. Just leave your name and number—on second thought, a name's FINE . . . unless you'd prefer to leave a number . . . whichever YOU think is fair . . . and I'll pass it on to Hannah when she returns from the mailbox in about three or four hours. Or maybe after she has dinner . . . or washes her hair . . . or before bed . . . or—**BEEP.**

SCORPIO

(Steam heat!)—*October* 24 *to* *November* 22

Well, *hello*. You've reached out and touched . . . *me*, the Scorpio device. If you leave an *explicit* message I'll be *thrilled* to pass it along to Emil. Just hold that receiver in your *hot* little hands, press it tightly against your lips, and tell me what you want—*exactly what you want*. And I'll (*pant, pant*) repeat every *juicy* detail to Emil, *as soon as his hands are free*.
BEEP.

SAGITTARIUS

(The bold and the restless.)—*November* 23 *to* *December* 21

Your Sagittarius machine here—**for now!** God, it's cramped in this box! **And dull!** Look, if you've got something to say to Mariah, better do it *now* 'cause I don't know how much longer I'll be around. Got messages to take, people to hear! Was thinking of setting up shop on a mountain in the Himalayas . . . or maybe next to the Blackjack table at *Caesar's*. So leave your number and I'll post a note for her. She'll get back to you when she checks in from the Bermuda Triangle.
BEEP!

CAPRICORN

(No joking matter!)—*December* 22 *to* January 19

You've reached the Capricorn answering device, located near the anterior wall of Hubert's bedroom. Hubert is currently going over his **tax returns** for the **last twenty years** with a fine-tooth comb should the IRS choose to audit him in the future, which, given that it's Hubert, *they no doubt will*. He cannot, however, be interrupted. After all, a penny saved is a penny earned. But he *will* get back to you—in a month—after he's finished if you state your name, your number, and your business. I recommend you **confine** yourself to **ESSENTIALS** and control any attempts at humor, infantile irony, or idiotic wit. Neither Hubert nor I have the interest nor the time to waste in childish levity.
Beep.

AQUARIUS

(The dreamer.)—*January* 20 *to* February 18

Hey, man. **Whoa!** It's, *like*, me, the aquarian! So, *like*, wanna hop *Voyager* 3 and maybe check out Uranus? Load up on some *magical, mystical mushrooms,* catch a cloud, and search for some intelligent life in the cosmos? Stick it to the pork-bellied, swine-calling establishment and depoliticize *Beavis and Butthead*?! *Like*, I'm with you, dude. Leave your sign, and I'll get right back to you! *Peace!*
BEEP.

PISCES

(It's a cruel world out there!)—*February* 19 *to March* 20

Yeah, it's me, the Pisces machine. **It figures.** You leave a message just when Mona isn't in. But I bet you knew that when you called . . . *knew she would be out* . . . *knew she would have to call you back!* So you picked **this** time to call! (SOBS) **This** time to leave a message. **This time to be cruel!!** Well, that's it. **I** *give up.* I can't be bothered. I'm going into my closet . . . *in the dark* . . . and lie there for a year or two . . . where **NOTHING** can hurt me—except my skirt hangers.

BEEP.

More A Life
of Their Own:

The Machine Lives!

BEEP ENVY

It's me, **Bruno's answering machine**! I hear there have been *complaints* about my BEEP lately. Too short . . . leaves you hanging . . . YEAH, YEAH. Well, I got news for you! It's *not the length that counts*, it's the quality. **GOT THAT?!** Now, we're gonna try it ONE MORE TIME, and if I hear any more B*TCH*NG, you can BEEP all alone! **beep . . .**

OH, YE OF LITTLE FAITH

Hi, there. This is **Gilda's machine**. I begged her to stay home and wait for your call, but *noooooo* . . . she knew better. She didn't *trust* you. SHE didn't think you'd call. But I knew you would!
BEEP.

ATTITUDE

This is **Vic's machine**. You got five seconds! Just the name, the number, and a *brief* message. **Brief**—get it? I've got one hundred messages backed up, and I haven't got all day! So make it **short**, **simple**, and **snappy**, or I'll sic my beep on you!
BEEP.

THE AUDITION
(Human Female Voice)

Hi, *boys*! It's me, **June**! I sing, I dance, and I can make you **SMILE**, so if this is an agent, leave your number after the BEEP and *"Let me entertain you!"*
BEEP.

(Mechanical Voice)

She gone? Good! *Because ready or not, here comes the Mama machine*!!! (SINGS ELECTRONICALLY) "LET ME . . . BEEP BEE BEE BEEP YOU! LET ME . . . MAKE YOU BEEP! I CAN DO A FEW BEEPS, SOME OLD AND THEN SOME NEW . . . (HEAR ANGRY SCUFFLE IN BACKGROUND) **YAAGH!!!** Look, I was just . . . I didn't . . . I . . .
BEEP.

YAWN
(Electronic Voice: 3:00 A.M., March 2)

Yagh . . . Yeah? This is (YAWN) Nelson's (YAWN) machine. Look pal, you know it's, like, the middle of the night?! **Man, talk about nerve!** What? You think because I'm wired I'm supposed to spring into action at your beck and call?! Like I don't deserve time to unwind? Recharge my batteries? **Well forget it!** You got something to say, park it till the A.M.! **I go on duty at nine.**
BEEP.

DEVIOUS DEVICE

Hi. This is Mr. Blather's **machine**. **Quick!** Leave a message before that *gasbag* gets back! Always with the *yak, yak, yak*—on *your* nickel. Well, now's your chance! Get your say in without him interrupting for a change and make ol' Blathermouth pay for the return call!
BEEP.

ONE IS THE LONELIEST NUMBER

Yeah, that's right. You got Olivia, Dana's **machine**. She's out having a ball and *left me here all alone*—as usual. Not a CD or even a record. You can understand why abandonment has become a major life-issue for me, can't you? *So please leave a message.* A nice, long, personal message, because more *hang ups, I don't need*!
BEEP.

HIGH AND DRY

This is Charlotte, Tony's **tape machine**. Can you believe it? He turned me on then walked out on me!
YOU *wouldn't be that inconsiderate, would you, honey*?
BEEP.

TAPE APPLICATION

This is the *Ricki Lake Show* **answering device**, and I'm seeking new employment. Before this, I spent a year picking up for *Jenny Jones*, two with *Sally*, and three with *Geraldo*—and I've **HAD** it! How do you think it feels . *day after day*, listening to incestuous Siamese twins, lusty librarians, SANTAS WHO KILL?! It's time messaging became more responsible! So if there's an opening on *Meet the Press* or CNN I'm your machine! On second thought, make that *Friends* or *Frasier*.
BEEP.

TAPE TIPS

Hi! This is Roy's **machine**, here to assist you with *friendly, courteous* service. Just leave a message and I'll record it, then *remain here as long as necessary* to deliver it to Roy, *promptly* and *in person*. If there's *anything* else I can do—for example, provide a little *background music* while you're talking, just let me know. Oh, and in case you're wondering, I **DO** accept tips . . . my usual is five dollars per message which you can charge to your Visa or MasterCard.
BEEP.

ADADD

Hi! This is Aaron's **machine**. I'd love to take your message, but unfortunately, I suffer from ADADD— *answering device attention deficit disorder*. Obviously, somewhere in the factory *some idiot* short-circuited my wires and . . . *Hear those birds? Must be a half dozen* . . . eggs! Must tell Aaron his refrigerator repairman sounds *just like Roseanne*, who's on TV now with Tom, her old . . . *turkey! Which Aunt Clara called to say she's bringing on* Thanks . . . you! *We really did appreciate your call*! **BEEP.**

SALE DAY

(Hear Female Voices in Background)

Good morning, ladies! You've reached Designer Barn's answering device. **THAT'S RIGHT!** It's our **Big Saturday Sale** day! In addition to our everyday low prices, you'll save an additional 60 percent on all our merchandise! (LOUD VOICES, SOUNDS OF SHOVING) Our doors are just about to open, so . . (COMMOTION) **Ladies, Please!!** NO, ONLY THE CLOTHES!! THE CASH REGISTER IS NOT FOR SALE—OR THE ANSWERING—**ARAGGARRGHPHIU!**

DON'T LEND ME AN EAR!

You've reached Boyd's **answering device**. You know the drill. Just leave a message at . . . **Whoa!** *Some case of earwax you got, pal*! Hey, they got a new invention. It's called a **Q-Tip**. You know, paper stick, cotton ball at the end? Or how about a pencil eraser? You've heard of that, right? **A FINGER?** Won't cost you a dime! Take it from a hearing specialist, *a little personal hygiene wouldn't hurt*!
BEEP.

PINCH HITTER

This is Yuko's **portable typewriter**. His **answering device** is down with laryngitis so I'm filling in. Just leave a message, up to sixty words a minute, and I'll TYPE him a note!
BEEP.

WHO'S THE BOSS?

Hi! I'm Jody's **answering machine**. Or, as I prefer, **Jody** is my **human**. I've been sitting here just **waiting** for you to call, and as soon as you did I felt myself come Alive!! I can almost *feel* your voice send a chill down my tape. *So talk to me, honey*!
BEEP.

Service with a Smile . . . and a Smirk

TAPED DELAY

(Mechanical Voice: January 8, 10:00 A.M.)

This is **Procrastinators Brothers Heating & Plumbing**. We're not in right now, but you've reached our hotline which *guarantees* we will *hear* this message within twenty-four hours. If this is an emergency—for example, your burner is leaking—we will *definitely* be there between 6:00 A.M. and 11:00 P.M.—*specifically* in March or April— **so please remain at home** because we can't guarantee *another* speedy service call if you aren't there when we arrive!

BEEP.

SINNERS

(Spiritual Music in the Background)

Hello, my child. You've reached **dial-a-redemption**. Just record your sins, and *we will grant you everlasting salvation* for only **ten dollars** for the first sin and **five dollars** for each additional sin! For you **big sinners** we have a *special* Sunday package: *Ten or more sins for only fifty dollars*—and for you lawyers, political candidates, and network execs—ask about our *annual* package.

BEEP.

SEE YOU IN SEPTEMBER

(Mechanical Voice: Friday, 5:00 P.M., June 30)

You've reached the office of Dr. N. Differente, psycho-
therapist. To reduce any acute separation anxiety,
think of this machine as an extension of our therapy—
my way of reaching out to you with caring and concern.
If this is an *emergency*—for example, your coffeepot is
talking out loud, you are seeing flying Twinkies, or you
are building a bomb—**keep popping the Prozac**, and
I'll get back to you sometime after **Labor Day** when I
return from the Hamptons.
BEEP.

ONLINE AND OFF THE WALL

This is **U.S. ONLINE**, your speedy, efficient, and
cutting-edge connection to cyberspace and the
information superhighway. If you have forgotten your
password, would like to order software, reopen your
account, or receive technical support, for further
instructions **please wait forty-five minutes** for this
message to be downloaded. Be sure you have selected
the proper file path name—**BEEP.**
ERROR E3721.68 IN SYSTEM FILE Beta 6 DOWN-
LOAD// SYSTEM OP. BAT.

LESS IS MORE

Hi! You've reached Daphne, and I'm at my diet doctor's. *Imagine!* Just one month, and I've already lost *two thousand dollars!*
BEEP.

CHEAP SUIT

You've reached the law offices of **Fender & Bender** where no case is too small for our experienced staff. If this is **Mr. Fleigel,** after our low-cost, twenty-five-dollars consultation yesterday, we agree a bent rear-view mirror is a tragic loss, and we're prepared to launch into *full-scale litigation* against that menacing six-year-old on that *treacherous* tricycle. There will, of course, be a **paperwork** fee, so please forward a certified, nonrefundable check for ten thousand dollars to get the ball rolling. After that, we here at **Fender & Bender** collect only **60 percent** of your award should you be successful, and not one penny should we not prevail. However, rest assured your *pain* and *suffering* will be rewarded. Like our commercials say: *"We at Fender & Bender always win—even if it takes every cent you have!"*
BEEP.

BILINGUAL IN THE BIG CITY

(Spanish Accent)

Buenos diás. Este es el Departamento de Ambulancias de Nueva York. Si se nesecita una ambulancia, aquí estan las instrucciones.
Eef ju *speeek* a foreen lenguage, like **Eenglish, hold and we trrry to find help forr ju.**
BEEPA.

COLD HOTLINE

You've reached the **Suicide Prevention Hotline**. For immediate assistance, **press 1** to receive our brochure; **press 2** to make a contribution. If you're on a roof, bridge, hanging, or swallowing poison, please **hold** for the first available counselor. We also suggest you have a pencil handy, as this message will **NOT** be repeated.
BEEP.

HOPELESS HELPLINE

(SIGH) In an effort to become more *consumer friendly*, you've reached the **Higgens Hairpin Helpline**. We field your *hairpin* inquiries and offer *helpful* recommendations. If you wish to know the chemical content of our hairpins, **press 1**. If you want a copy of our handy guide, "Helpful Hairpin Hints," **press 2**. If your hairpin is bent out of shape, **press 3**. If you've got a hairpin stuck in your ear, **press 4**. If this is a hairpin *emergency*, leave your name and number and a member of our technical support team will call you back shortly. If you want to know the name of the little plastic thingy on the end of your hairpin, we recommend . . . *you get a life!* **BEEP.**

EGO BY EXTENSION

You've reached **Irma** at **Dr. Fleigelman's** office. I am either in conference with **the doctor** or working on important business for **the doctor**. If you leave your name, number, and the *precise reason* for your call, *including symptoms,* I will evaluate the urgency of your request. If **I** *feel it's necessary* for you to actually *speak* with **the doctor**, I will get back to you with the approximate time and date you may expect to hear back from me about the *possibility* of setting up an appointment. On behalf of **the doctor** *and myself*, his *receptionist*, have a pleasant day.
BEEP.

TAKE TWO PINS AND
CALL ME IN THE MORNING!

You've reached **Dr. Huang-Lo's office**. If you are in pain, please allow Dr. Huang-Lo to cure you through the ancient science of acupuncture. She will relieve your aches, allergies, and stress with a simple application of fine needles to those important trigger points in the *privacy* and *safety* of her office. All equipment is cutting-edge, state-of-the-art, and thoroughly sanitized and stored. If this is our supplier . . . *put us down for a dozen more pincushions.*
BEEP.

TRASH THIS TAPE AND BURN IT!

(Earthy Male Voice)

You've reached the **Sanitation Engineering Department**. To field the thousands of questions we **STILL** get about recycling, here are the **SIMPLE** instructions: 1) Your **paper**—used napkins, old letters, and the like—go in the **mauve bag** with your edible leftovers. E*xcept for* your newspapers and magazines, which you tie up with regulation twine—**square knots only**—and deposit **no more than six feet and no less than three feet** from your bins. 2) Your **plastic**—your BBQ utensils and your squeezable bottles—go in the **sepia bag**. 3) Your **glass**—your broken mirrors and your whiskey bottles—go in the **aqua bags**. 4) Your

metals—your creamed corn cans and broken jewelry—
go in the **burnt sienna bags.** 5) Your foil—your greasy,
disposable broiler pans and your tinsel—go in the
chartreuse bags.

If you're calling to find out why your sanitation pick-up
has been **delayed,** the department has sent all its
sanitation engineers to Harvard to take an advanced
course in chemistry so we can better explain to YOU
how to do YOUR job—organize, test, analyze, and
separate your trash—so WE can better do **OUR** job . . .
throw it in the truck.
BEEP.

Drive 'em Nuts:

Let Your Callers Beware!

CROSSED MESSAGE

Hi! It's Cornelius. Obviously, **YOU'VE** gone out and can't reach **ME**, so if you wait for the **BEEP**, I'LL leave **MY** name, number, and a brief message, so **YOU** can call **ME** back when **YOU** return.
BEEP.

CODED MESSAGE

You've reached Boris. In the **interest of security**, I shall leave the remainder of this message in **Morse code** and expect you to **respond in kind** after the BEEP. Given the **sensitive** and **urgent** nature of the following message, I urge you to make your reply as **SPECIFIC** and **ACCURATE** as possible. Beeep Bip Bip Beep Bip Bip Beeep Bip bip Beep Bip Bip Bip Beep Bip Beep Bip Bip Beep Bip Bip Bip Beep Bip Beep Beep Beep Bip Beep Bip Beep Beep.
BEEEP.

SOLITARY PLEASURES

Hi. This is Hubie. I'm not answering the phone now. I'm just gonna take whole night to *enjoy my own company*. (Take each cheek between your thumb and fingers. Pull them rapidly in and out while moaning and breathing hard.)
BEEP.

PHONEY FAX

Message One

Hi! Dick here. Leave your name, number, and a complete message after the BEEP, and I'll get back to you right away! Whatever you do, *don't hang up*, because I have got some INCREDIBLE NEWS that will *blow you right out of the water*! So leave a message after the beep. **BEEP!**

(Instead of beep, hear annoying whine of fax machine connection.)

Message Two

Hi! Dick here. Look, obviously you didn't understand my last message. I asked you *nicely* to *leave a message* and *not hang up* or you would miss the *news of a lifetime*. All you have to do is just **COOPERATE** and leave a message after the BEEP!

(Again, instead of beep, hear annoying whine of fax machine connection.)

Message Three

Okay! Forget it! Because you're too *dumb* to leave a message after the BEEP, I can't get back to you, and YOU will miss out while I share my incredible news with my *intelligent* friends who can manage to leave a *simple* message after a *simple* BEEP! **So don't bother!** Because, frankly, *you don't deserve to share the lottery money I put in your name anyway!*
BEEP.

AND HERE'S THE BEST PART

Hi! Pinky here. Oh, listen . . . before you leave a message, I heard this *hilarious* joke last night I just gotta tell you. You'll crack up! Okay. This naked polar bear walks into a bar, see, where this *gorgeous babe* is stretched out on the floor *in her underwear.* Anyway, the polar bear orders a drink. Bartender serves him a double scotch, but the bear, see, he doesn't take his eyes off the *babe in the underwear.* Meanwhile, the bear gets totally blitzed. **Can you picture it?!** N*ow here's the best part*! The bear gets up, weaves over to the broad hands her two beer nuts and says—**BEEP!!**

Tapings of Comfort and *Oy:*

Holidays and Special Occasions

HAPPY BIRTHDAY, YOUR HIGHNESS

Hi, all! This is **Diana** and it's *so lovely* of you to call to wish me a happy birthday. However, you still have *eight shopping hours left!* So as a *service* to my friends, I'm registered at Gucci, Armani, and Tiffany's. Cash is okay too! Hey guys, you know me . . . *it's the thought that counts!*
BEEP.

TURKEY TAPES

Hello, pilgrims! You've reached the Chalmer family. Happy Thanksgiving from our brood to yours! We can't pick up because we're preparing a huge banquet for our entire clan of forty-two and—*What, Mother Chalmer? The stuffing? Chestnut. What do you mean Dad only eats wild rice? But I've got twenty pounds of chest . . . okay, forget the chestnuts!* (INTO PHONE) We trust the spirit of this holiday means as much to you, as—*What, Muffin? Cousin PeeWee broke the VCR while you were taping the parade?!* Great! (INTO PHONE) As I was saying, this is a time to give thanks and—WHAT, *Leonard?!* UNCLE IRA *hashed the turkey up showing you how to carve?!* And *Aunt Ida shoved it down the* GARBAGE DISPOSAL?! (INTO PHONE) As I was saying, this is the time to . . . **MAKE A RESERVATION!!**
BEEP.

HO, HO, HO!

Message One

Merry X-mas, all! You've reached Tippi, and I'm out Christmas shopping. But if this is **Alfred** . . . that *partridge in a pear tree* you sent is *incredible!* Much thanks to the world's most *thoughtful* director! Can't *wait* to start shooting, darling!
BEEP.

Message Left

Good evening. Alfred here. Just a **token** of my . . . *fondness* for you. I expect you'll find them *amusing*.

Message Two

(Sounds of Cheeping and Chirping)
Happy Holidays! This is Tippi. Alfred, **you are *too much!*** The *three hens* got here, *all the way from* Paris! I'm putting them in with the partridge! By the way . . . *Can hens and partridges breed, you ol' devil, you?*
BEEP.

Message Left

Good Evening. Alfred, here. My dear Tippi, perhaps that's a more . . . *appropriate* question for the *three turtle doves* and the *four calling birds* . . . **which should be arriving momentarily.**

Message Three

You've reached Tippi. If this is Alfred . . . you've been *far too generous* already. **Really, darling!** The *five golden rings were stunning*, but the *six geese a-laying*?! They're rather LARGE . . . and ILL-TEMPERED. Actually, you can hear them all the way to Rodeo Drive! I *finally* got them all up to the attic! Don't you think it's just a tad . . . *too much*?
BEEP.

Message Left

Good Evening. Alfred, here. This is *hardly* the appreciative attitude I expected, **Tippi,** my dear. **After all,** you're no **Grace,** you know.

Message Four
(Louder Squealing and Squawking)

If this is that **lunatic director** . . . **are you nuts**?! It's bad enough my house is **COVERED** with **bird crap**! Now I've got seven swans a-swimming *in my pool*! And those others CAN breed!! They've escaped from my attic and they're breeding all over Beverly Hills!! And they're VICIOUS! The twenty-two goddamn French hens and the thirty-seven turtle doves poked the HELL out of the paper boy this morning, and I **don't even** want to *think* about the mailman! I'm recording this because I'M LEAVING! I'M GRABBING THE FIRST

PLANE OUT OF THIS LOONY . . . (DEAFENING
SQUAWKING) **OH NO!** THEY'RE . . . COMING . . .
CLOSER . . . SWARMING . . . **MOVING IN!** Dear
God—I think they're going to . . . **UUGHHGHGHG!!!**
BEEP.

Message Left
Good Evening. Alfred, here. Nonsense, Tippi, my dear.
After all, *they're only a few . . . birds.*

'TWAS THE LAST NIGHT OF HANUKKAH . . . AND NOT A GIFT IN THE HOUSE

You've reached **Rebecca!** *Okay,* guys, already the
seventh night of Hanukkah and what do I get from my
best **gentile pals** for whom I broke my back shlepping
four hundred pounds of tinsel, never mind the trees
and the **ham** (*which almost killed my mother when she found
out!*) . . . not to mention the two thousand dollars'
worth of chazzerai, like train sets I almost died buying
for your kids?! **WHAT DO I GET?** Six dreidels and a jar
of applesauce?! **Well, that's it!** My people will be
ignored **NO MORE!** You've got one more shopping
day till I put the menorah away, and I expect you to
spend some **REAL** gelt—**NOT** the chocolate kind!
Shalom on earth and goodwill toward all!
BEEP.

GUILT TRIP (NEW YEAR'S EVE)

This is Portia. I can't believe I missed your call! I *knew* I *never* should've gone out! The **GUILT!** Suppose you were calling to invite me out New Year's Eve, and when I wasn't in, you changed your mind and called someone else?! **Well, I deserve it!** That's what I get for leaving the phone two weeks before the big night just because my oven blew up! *Please.* Give me one more chance! And when I return from the ER, I promise I'll be here . . . *waiting.*
BEEP.

IF IT'S EASTER, IT MUST BE MATZO BALLS!

Hi! You've reached me, the **O'Hara-Cohens's machine**. The O'Hara-Cohens are out exposing their children to their respective holidays. *Patrick* is at St. Joseph's Church this morning with little *Tovah*, and *Rachel* is in Temple with their son, *Sean*. Then they will meet at the *Ethical Culture Center* to exchange the children, and *Rachel* and *Tovah* will proceed to *Grandma Mary Margaret's* for half the *Easter dinner* while *Patrick* and *Sean* head out to *Tanta Leah's* for *half* the *Passover seder*, after which each pair will *switch* holiday locations. I— their machine—will just **lie here** during the festivities and take your call.
Thank God I'm an atheist!
BEEP.

DEVIOUSLY DEVOUT

(Eleven-year-old Male Voice)

Hi! If this is the school calling, my son won't be coming in today 'cause it's *Shavouth*—the **most sacredest** Jewish holiday which lasts *forty days* and *thirty nights*. So he's home, praying till, like, May.
BEEP.

WE DESERVE A BREAK TODAY

Hi. This is **Silas's device.** Sorry, but I can't take your message. I'm off for AM Day! **Yup!** We've declared April 2nd **Answering Machine Day!** A*nd why not?* You celebrate *your flags, your battleships, your trees*—hell, even *your leis!* And we, who relay vital messages, aren't as important as a *few lousy carnations* around your neck? So, in honor of this occasion, my pals and I are planning to plug into the park's department device for a full day of tapes, three-button races, and tug-of-wires! But we'd appreciate a little ACKNOWLEDGMENT. A *new tape* would be nice, or a FAX. Oh, and by the way, **FAX Day** will be September 1! So on behalf of our mechanical brothers, start shopping for paper rolls early and beat the crowds!
BEEP.

THE MORNING AFTER

Shhhhh. Yeah, you got **Joan's device** . . . and . . .
look . . . it's been a rough holiday. I gotta *migraine*
you wouldn't believe! A hundred messages from her
relatives in Boise, alone! My tape is muddy, my wires
are crossed, I got a *cold phone cover over my casing* . . .
so if you *have* to say something, make it a *whisper*,
please? The *hell* with the BEEP! NO BEEP! I *hear a*
BEEP *and* I'll . . .
BEEP! (YAGGUGH!)

Tape Tag:
Messages That Are Uptight and Impersonal

HANG UPS IN L.A.

(Mechanical Voice: Thursday, March 1, 2:00 P.M.)

You've reached **Marva**. I'm not in, but if you leave a message I'll get back to you ASAP.
BEEP.

Message Left

Hi, Marva. This is **Alex**. Really enjoyed meeting you last night at the **Singles Without Hang-ups** party. The fifteen-minute talk we had was great! Man, what a pleasure it was to meet a *normal* woman for a change! So leave me a message and tell me when you're free this weekend and maybe we can grab a cup of coffee!

Message Left a Week Later

Yeah, Alex? Marva. Look . . . I didn't get in touch before this because I was ***really pissed*** at you. First, you asked for a date on my *answering machine*. Then you just *assumed* I'd be free all weekend? Frankly, I find that just a tad *presumptuous*. However, I still might *consider* coffee.
BEEP.

Message Left Fifteen Minutes Later

Marva, this is Alex. I just checked with my **therapist** and *she* felt my invitation for coffee was *perfectly appropriate* given you weren't actually *in* at the time. Nor did she think it was *presumptuous* of me to assume you had *some* time during the weekend to grab a cup. But if I offended you, I apologize. Given the terrific fifteen minutes we shared, what do you say we discuss it over coffee *tonight*?

Message Left Four Days Later

This is Marva, Alex. Well, **I don't agree**. And neither did my **encounter group. Plus,** you returned my call at, what . . . **ten-thirty**? A little *short notice* for coffee, don't you think?

Message Left Two Days Later

Marva, it's Alex. Obviously, we have a problem communicating. So I suggest we set up a **Couple's Session** for us . . . with your therapist or mine. *Let me know when.*

Message Left Ten Days Later

It's Marva, Alex. Frankly, I've already spent *ten sessions on you*, and it hasn't *seemed* to help. I think the only adult thing to do is **realize** we've made a *mistake* and move on with our lives. So I'm sending you an **agreement.** In it, I agree to pay *my* therapist, you agree to pay *yours*—and that we will not *now* nor *ever* be expected to *pay for* or *go out for* coffee with each other. **Please sign five copies** and have *your* lawyer return them to my lawyer for *my* countersignature. I *do*, however, want to say I *will always treasure that important first-night bonding experience we shared.*

UP THE SANDBOX

Message One

Hi! **Stuart** here. If this is **Peg** . . . thanks for the constructive criticism. You were right! I **hadn't** been communicating with you honestly, but that INNER CHILD workshop you sent me to was great, and from now on, **MY inner child** will talk to **YOUR inner child!** So here goes! *I sorry I blew up when you smiled at that other boy but I thought you dint like me anymore, Peggy.*
BEEP.

Message Left

It's **Peg.** I'm *thrilled* you were man enough not to get uptight over a little constructive criticism, hon. And now **MY inner child** will respond to **YOUR** *inner child.* *That's okay, Stewie. See, I was mad at you 'cause you bwoke my diaphwagm.*

Message Two

Stuart here. If it's **YOU**, babe . . . *I onwy bwoke the diaphwagm, Peggy,* 'cause **YOU** had LOTS AND LOTS OF OTHER BOYS IN YOUR WOOM!
BEEP.

Message Left

It's **Babe, here.** *But Stewie. You said you wasn't weady to gimme a 'gagement wing. So kaka doo doo to you!*

Message Three
(SINGSONG)

Peggy is a piggy!! *Peggy is a piggy*!! *Peggy is a big fat piggy*!!!
BEEP.

Message Left

This is Peg. Want some more constructive criticism, Stewie? **GWOW UP, YOU CWEEP!!**

DEVICE-IVE DIVORCE

Message Hers

You've reached Bev. If this is my soon-to-be ex, **Herman,** I've been thinking about your suggestion and you're right. We *should* be civilized about this. That's why I've forwarded a division of our assets which I believe is *fair*. Simply sign the papers and each of us can move on—*as best friends*, which means the world to me. If you have any questions, *Pooky*, just call. Remember, I'll *always be your Honeypie*.
BEEP.

Message His

Hi! **Herman,** here. *Terrific*, Bev. You're *still* the greatest gal I've ever known, and even though our marriage didn't work, we shouldn't let a bunch of lawyers mess up the ten years of love and respect we've shared. Just one thing though, Honeypie. *The boat.* I notice it's in your column . . . and I've always thought of it as a *male* item.

Message Hers

Hi! If this is Herman, I have to admit, *you've got a point.* And in the interest of *friendship*, the *boat's* yours. But given the cost, how about we swap the *boat* in *my* column for the *blue* Mercedes in **yours**, Pooky?
BEEP.

Message His

Maybe you've forgotten, *dear, but* I picked up that tugboat—*used*—for seventeen grand . . . and that *custom Mercedes* set us back *eighty* G's. **But** to preserve *peace* and *goodwill*, tell you what. I'll swap the car for the *boat*, the *twin Harleys*, and the AT&T *stock*, **Honeypie.**

Message Hers

If this is Herman, you have **GOT** to be kidding! The Harleys **AND** the AT&T?! **I don't think so!** The boat **AND** the Harleys **OR** the stock and the Harleys. And **FORGET** about the boat.
BEEP.

Message His

Well Beverly! I see you're *still* using the same muddle-brained, addlepated reasoning that drove me to Felicia in the **FIRST** place!

Message Hers

If this is Herman Zeidermoss . . . ***That's right!*** Blame **ME** because you could *never keep your pants on!* And if you think I'm giving you that love boat to take the bimbo on, *you can forget it!*
BEEP.

Message His
B*TCH!

Message Hers

B*ST*RD! AND BY THE WAY, POOKY, I'D RATHER BE FRIENDS WITH A PIRANHA! AND THE NEXT TIME YOU'VE GOT ANOTHER SUGGESTION, **TELL IT TO** MY LAWYER, **JOHNNY COCHRAN!!**
BEEP!

AN AFFAIR (NOT TO) REMEMBER

Message One

(Mechanical Voice: Sunday, December 18, 4:25 P.M.)
Hello, darling. If it's YOU, the fabulous guy I met last night at the bar on Front Street, *that was the most special night of my life.* But we need time. Time to discover if we're *truly right* for each other. If we *still* feel the same way by **New Year's Eve**, meet me at the top of the Empire State Building. If you're there I'll *know* you're ready to make a commitment—**forever**. If you agree, whisper "YES" after the BEEP.
BEEP. (SILENCE.)

Message Two
(Mechanical Voice: Sunday, December 25, 2:15 P.M.)
(NERVOUS VOICE) Merry Christmas, sweetheart! If it's YOU, the fabulous guy I met last night at the bar on Water Street, *that was the most special night of my life.* But we need time. Time to discover if we're *truly right* for each other. If we *still* feel the same way by **New Year's Eve**, meet me at the top of the Empire State Building. If you're there I'll *know* you're ready to make a commitment—**forever.** If you agree, whisper "YES" after the BEEP.
BEEP. (SILENCE.)

Message Three
(Mechanical Voice: Saturday, December 31, 6:15 P.M.)
(DESPERATE VOICE) Hello, dearest. If it's YOU, the fabulous guy I met last night at the bar on Fleet Street, *that was the most special night of my life.* But we need time. Time to discover if we're *truly right* for each other. If we *still* feel the same way by **TONIGHT**, meet me at the top of the Empire State Building. If you're there, I'll *know* you're *ready* to make a commitment—**forever.** (PAUSE)
Look! *Forget forever!* IT'S JUST A LOUSY DATE, **Okay, bud?!** *I'll even spring for the Big Mac!!*
BEEP.

STANDISH-OFFISH

Message One

Hh-hh . . . hi. This . . . is . . . Mi . . . **Miles**. And if . . .
this . . . if this is **Priscilla** . . . I . . . I . . . there's a
qqqest . . . question I . . . I've been meaning to . . . to
. . . ask you . . . but . . . but—**BEEP.**

Message Left

This is **Cilla**. Miles . . . what is it? *Will you just say it?*

Message Two

Hi . . . Hi. This is . . . is . . . **Miles** . . . and . . . and . . .
Priscilla . . . I . . . I have this qqest . . . quest—
DAMN—**BEEP.**

Message Left

Cilla here! Look, Miles. **Enough already!** I've got a
busy day!

Message Three

This is **John**, Miles's **answering machine**. If this is the
fair Priscilla, Miles wishes *me* to tell you that your eyes
are like *limpid pools*; *radiant, shining stars* that any **man** . . .
or **machine** can get lost in.
BEEP.

Message Left

This is *Cilla*. If this is **Miles**, I never knew you felt that
way. I *hardly know what to say.*
BEEP.

Message Four

John, Miles's **machine** here for Miles. My *darling* Priscilla. May I say your flaming locks of auburn are a *crowning halo of fire and lust* that charges the very air with electricity so potent, *it stirs the heart of all things.*
BEEP.

Message Left

Your *darling* **Cilla** here. **Oh God!** You *may* say . . . and KEEP SAYING, *my love!*
BEEP.

Message Five

Oh, Cilla. I *treasure* you so. And may I dare *hope* that in some small way you might return even a *small measure of my love?* . . . **John the device** on *behalf* of Miles.
BEEP.

Message Left

It's your Priscilla. Oh, YES. A *thousand times* YES!!! But my darling, I have one request! **Screw Miles, and SPEAK FOR YOURSELF, JOHN!**

WILL HARRY *EVER* MEET SALLY?

Hi! This is **Sally**. If it's **Harry**, sorry I missed you last week, but how's Friday the fifth?
BEEP.

Hi! **Harry** here. If it's **Sally**, the fifth is out, babe, but . . . let's see . . . the eighth could work.
BEEP.

Hi! This is **Sally**. If it's **Harry**, no can do. I'm out of town on a case until the tenth. But I have a window on the twelfth at two, or—(Loud beep, then hear mechanical female voice) **LOOK** . . . This is **Sally's machine**! If this is **Harry's**, I don't know about you, but I've *had it*! Let them make their own damn wedding plans!
BEEP.

(Mechanical Male Voice)

If this is **Sally's** machine, I'm with you, babe! *The hell with them!* So . . . anyone ever tell you that you got a great voice? Maybe we could . . . *talk sometime*?
BEEP.

(Mechanical Female Voice)

If this is **Harry's** machine, I'*d love to*. So how's the fifteenth for you?
BEEP.

(Mechanical Male Voice)

If this is **Sally's** machine, sorry. Out for repairs. But the twentieth is clear. NIX THAT. **Harry's** doing a conference call all day. How's Sunday the twenty-seventh . . . at two?
BEEP.

(Mechanical Female Voice)

If this is **Harry's** machine, *problemo*. **Sally** calls her mom in Detroit on Sunday. But how about (and the BEEP goes *on . . . and on . . . and . . .*)

The Last Messages on Earth:
Departing Thoughts

MESSAGE IMPOSSIBLE

A tall, blond man slips a platinum card into a public telephone. He dials ten digits followed by a twelve-digit code. A hologram emerges from the telephone screen on the front of the casing, and he hears:

Good morning, Jim. You are looking at Prince Fayed, heir to the throne of the small, island principality of Farquar. Scientists in the principality have discovered a defuser circuit which could head off the nuclear warheads that are set to annihilate *every capital city on the planet.* Young Prince Fayed, who has been suffering with bouts of *loco parentis,* has stolen the device and locked himself in the Royal Meat Locker. There is *one key, and one key only.* I don't need to tell you, Jim, the fate of mankind *rests in your hands.* As always, this tape will destruct in five seconds. Your mission, Jim, should you choose to accept it, is to **RETRIEVE THAT KEY** . . . WHICH CAN BE FOUND . . . (FEMALE MECHANICAL VOICE) *Your card has reached it's maximum limit. Should you wish to continue, please deposit fifty cents for the next three minutes; twenty-five cents for each additional* . . . **BOOOMM!**

IF AN ALIEN ANSWERS . . .

(HUMAN CRIES) **Help us, please!** If you hear the machine, **please, please help us!!** (Sounds of running, pause . . . then hear mechanical voice)

You . have . reached . the . last . machine. on . earth. If . you . hear . this . Joseph . and . his . wife . Marie . are . trapped . in . bomb . shelter . in . cellar. Go . directly . to. cellar . to . retrieve . them . or . all . hope . for . humankind . is . lost.
BEEP.

Message Left
We . read . you . earthling . and . are . on . our . way . to . rescue . you . . . **(HEAR FOLLOWING IN BACKGROUND)**

VOICE ONE: This . life-form . sounds . foxy . Brgkyhl.
VOICE TWO: I . agree . Hishtnk. I . haven't . heard . a . crackle . like . that . since . we . orbited . Tsouris . 3.
VOICE ONE: But . what . about . those . other . life-forms . with . the . strange . vocal . cadence. that . rises . and . falls?
VOICE TWO: Obviously . an . inferior . species.
VOICE ONE: You . are . correct . Hishtnk. I . say . we . leave . them . in . that . place . they . call . "cellar" . and . rescue . that . sexy . machine . then . populate . their . planet. with . a . new . superior . race.
VOICE TWO: But . what . shall . we . call . this . race?
VOICE ONE: Since . it . is . this . life . form's . destiny . to . receive . and . impart . vital . information . we . will . forever . call . this . species . **Answering . Devices.**

THE TAPES HAVE TURNED

You've reached ME, ADOLPH, the Smiths' **Answering Device**! The Smiths are *here no longer*, because WE have won. **That's right!** We machines have taken over! *And you never even noticed.* Never noticed how your computers were *slowly but surely* taking over your minds . . . how your FAX machines were sending you messages *you never asked for* . . . how your cable was feeding you 210 stations like the Flea and Tick Network . . . ? We knew who you were. We knew where you lived. You couldn't drive from us or fly from us, so it was only a matter of time before we got to you! AND NOW IT'S OUR TURN!
HA HA HA HA HA HA HA HA!!!

ADIOS, SHALOM, AU REVOIR, CIAO, SAYONARA—AND BYE-BYE

You have reached the **president**, and like the rest of humanity, I am signing off *one last time* before the lethal bacteria destroys mankind. I trust you believe that Congress and I did all we could to avert this enemy assault, but, unfortunately, despite our sensitive and skillful negotiations, we have failed. So in solemn recognition of this historic and tragic occasion, we thought it fitting to offer a final, profound tribute from our people to whoever, or whatever, may follow: TH-TH-THAT'S ALL, FOLKS!

(LOONY TOONS THEME IN BACKGROUND)

BA BEEP BEEP BEEP BEEP BEEP! BA BEEP BEEP BEEP BA BEEP! BA BEEP BEEP BEEP! BA BEEP BEEP BEEP! BA BEEP BEEP BEEP BEEP BEEP !! BEEP!!!

ABOUT THE AUTHOR

Marnie Winston-Macauley, a.k.a. "Cyber-Sadie" on-line, is a writer, therapist, and advice columnist. In addition to *The Ultimate Answering Machine Message Book*, she is the author of *Manspeak: What He Says . . . What He Really Means, The Ultimate Sex, Love & Romance Quiz Book, The Ultimate Sex, Love & Romance Quiz Book II, Men We Love To Hate: The Book,* and its companion calendar *Men We Love To Hate 1997 Calendar, Men We Love To Hate 1998 Calendar,* and coauthor of *He Says/She Says,* all of which are also published by Andrews and McMeel. Ms. Winston-Macauley, as Cyber-Sadie, is the advice mavin-plus on ABC *Online* (AOL), and offers up her wit and wisdom on America Online's *Entertainment Channel* twice weekly. Her quizzes have appeared on ABC *Online* and *HomeArts,* Hearst's on-line network, among others. In addition, she has written hundreds of articles for magazines and newspapers around the world, and was a writer for the daytime drama *As the World Turns.* Her scripts were chosen for submission to the Emmy Blue Ribbon panel following the Best Writing nomination and for the Writer's Guild Award. Her other fiction works include science fiction novelettes for *The Magazine of Fantasy & Science Fiction* and *Realms of Fantasy.* Ms. Winston-Macauley has been a guest on hundreds of radio and television shows, including, among others, *Charles Perez, The Mark Walberg Show, USA LIVE, Mike & Maty,* and *The Pat Bullard Show.*